An Improbable Journey
A Story of Courage and Enterprise

By

Karna Dev Bardhan

Copyright © 2023 by — Karna Dev Bardhan —All Rights Reserved.

It is not legal to reproduce, duplicate, or transmit any part of this document in either electronic means or printed format. Recording of this publication is strictly prohibited.

Table of Contents

Foreword 1
Introduction 3
My Family 6
My Father – A Hero Who Made Me What I Am 15
The Telegram 21
Early Life: Adventures & Misadventures 25
Doon School (1951-1958) 27
School Holidays 30
Learning British History 33
Work Ethics 36
Six Early Life Lessons 38
Vellore 46
'Bring up the Bodies' 51
A Christmas Gift 53
Thirst – Yet Fearing Water 56
The Descent of Man 57
Grimace 59
Benign Britannia: British Soft Power 61
Oxford 64
Life in the Laboratory in My Early Days 67
The Odour of Nail Varnish Remover! 68
CPR 72
Sheffield 83
Bitter Almonds 85
The Driving Test 90

Rotherham	93
The Growth of Gastroscopy	97
The Question of Transfusion	108
Hypnosis in Gastroenterology	112
Domiciliary Visits	115
The Story of 'The Hut'	119
The Rigours and Romance of a Database	130
Bile Acids and the Small Intestine: Foe --- or Friend?	144
Some Interesting Patients' Stories	147
Mellow Yellow	151
A Peaceful Passing	156
Success: Illusion & Reality	159
The British Science Association (BSA)	166
A Personal Journey	170
Memories from Trips Abroad	189
The BRET Story	198
Projects Supported by BRET	204
Appendix	208

Foreword

An improbable journey in medicine is a unique story of one medical doctor's experience of arriving in the UK as a prestigious Rhodes Scholar in 1964 and the subsequent remarkable passage of his career thereafter.

Professor Bardhan is a hugely loved and admired figure in UK Gastroenterology. The story is told by Professor Bardhan in chronological order through a series of clinical vignettes.

Although this is one man's experience of the UK and the NHS from the 1960s onwards, the obstacles encountered and overcome along the way are relevant to any overseas doctor entering the NHS. As the story unfolds, the reader gets a real sense of the resilience that was required to progress through the ranks of hospital medicine in order to reach the hallowed post of becoming a Consultant.

In particular, this is a fascinating account through first-hand views of the evolving advances of gastroenterology, cardiac resuscitation and six decades of our NHS healthcare system that is still a national treasure.

As a result of Professor Bardhan's endeavours, Rotherham became a centre of excellence both nationally and internationally in gut medicine. Bridge chapels were established in medieval Europe with the purpose of offering spiritual comfort to travellers. The Chapel on the Bridge in Rotherham is widely viewed as England's best example of this and is described as a 'gem in the midst of Rotherham'. The same could be said of Professor Bardhan's spiritual relationship with the people of Rotherham. He took them into his heart and they reciprocated. It was this act, along with the omnipresent support of Gouri (Professor Bardhan's wife and a

Consultant Haematologist in her own right), that led to such unprecedented success.

The story is hugely entertaining and easy to read. One does not need to have a medical background to enjoy an improbable journey. What comes across most of all is the nature of the writer: an inquisitive, fun-loving, highly intelligent young man who becomes a gracious and beloved father figure in UK Gastroenterology. Despite all the hardships he faces throughout the journey, be it physical or professional, he retains a certain childlike innocence. For those of us who know him or have had the privilege to work for him, when reading this book you will feel that he is in the room beside you.

Professor David Sanders MB ChB, MD, FACG, FRCP

The Chapel on the Bridge, Rotherham

Introduction

Wednesday, 28 May 2014, morning: at the waterfalls, Great Falls, Virginia, USA

My wife Gouri and I were visiting our daughter Suchitra and her family at Great Falls in Virginia. One sunny day the delightful Danny and Cynthia Hourigan, our daughter's in-laws, kindly took us to the spectacular waterfalls just a few miles from Chris and Suchi's home. On the way back to the car, Danny took me to one side to have a conversation. Well aware that medical research is carried out in major teaching hospitals and universities, he asked out of genuine curiosity how gastroenterology could have blossomed in a small district general hospital to become recognised internationally.

I had never stopped to think how we managed to combine clinical work, research and teaching as it had seemed the natural thing to do. The greatest joy is not what I have been able to do but what our youngsters have gone on to achieve.

As I struggled to give a suitable answer, Danny suggested I write about it. The rest of the family reinforced this. A few days later we were back in Rotherham, and our son, Satyajeet, and my team members enthusiastically supported the idea.

Though 'almost retired', I was working close to full-time with ongoing research. Gouri volunteered to help me, as did members of my team. The final obstacle was how to write engagingly! Our group has published many papers, but these are in the language of medicine and science: dry, dusty and devoid of real-life excitement and emotion.

I approached the staff at Rotherham Library for guidance on writing, and they suggested contacting Ray Hearne, who ran a writers' group. I was pleasantly surprised when Ray phoned me and introduced himself a few days before I left for the USA to revisit my family. He told me briefly about the history of the writers' group and its parlous financial state now that Arts Council funding had been cut, which precluded taking on any new members. Nevertheless, he generously made an exception for me. I sensed Ray was an indomitable spirit, the sort of person I would like to engage with. We met up a few days later, and he suggested that whilst in the USA, I should try to write about my family as a warm-up exercise.

I reflected on how life and events in Rotherham had been truly amazing since joining as 'the new boy' on 10 January 1973, prematurely appointed, inexperienced and seemingly hopelessly out of my depth. Yet each of my endeavours began with a first step, and my team and I progressed. Sometimes a path was 'blocked', in the sense that further progress would take disproportionate time, interfering with my clinical responsibilities. Miraculously, however, another path would open!

I realised that my time in Rotherham was really an improbable journey, and I decided to put pen to paper.

Within a few weeks, however, the practical difficulties became apparent! I had never thought memoirs would feature in my life. Therefore, I was caught unprepared, as I had no written record of events! Incidents, people and topics started to 'telescope', and I could not fully recall the sequence of events.

I joined the writers' group, which met on average once a month when around ten of the many members would attend the session. I would draft an essay of about one thousand to eleven hundred words and then prepare a final version to read out to the group in about ten minutes at a comfortable speed. Importantly, I would collect feedback and make changes to the text. Gradually, I realised that writing memoirs is very different from reporting research work.

Life has been kind to me. Over the years, the efforts of our great team at Rotherham and the wonderful support I had from colleagues, former teachers and magnificent patients allowed us to grow and receive national and international recognition. I know nothing about 'management methods' but gradually realised that I could make better decisions when *everyone* gave me their view, irrespective of rank. Thus, I wanted to hear from the most junior, be they doctors or medical students, trainee nurses or auxiliary staff, as the latter are often in close company with the patient. My only role as the consultant, the 'boss' as it were, was to carry the can! It was the 'we together', aided by the kindness of strangers, which made growth possible.

This was the first time I tried to write something apart from research papers, and I sincerely hope that you will find some interest in the story of this improbable journey.

I would not have been able to go ahead with this project without the tremendous help of various people. I have received immense support from my devoted secretary Beverley Mason, the inspirational leader of the writers' group, Ray Hearne; my wife, Gouri; my patients; the hospital staff; my team members; and all the people who have allowed me to play a small part in their lives.

My Family

When our son Satyajeet was a teenager, he asked Gouri why I knew so little about my family while she knew so much about hers. This was a deep question, particularly from a youngster!

My knowledge is limited as I had lost connection with my forebears during forcible and often bloody migration when the Indian subcontinent was partitioned in 1947 into India and Pakistan. The native state of my family, Bengal, was split into West Bengal (India) and East Bengal (Pakistan). East Bengal later became Bangladesh. My family was drawn from both sides, and partition caused migration and dispersion of my relatives.

Gaps in knowledge widened because of premature deaths in both paternal and maternal branches of my family. My father was a doctor in the Army, so his life was 'semi-nomadic', characterised by frequent transfers at short intervals. To avoid disruption of education, a whole generation of my age and similar background was sent to boarding schools.

Of my immediate bloodline, only my sister, Madhu (Dr Madhumala Bardhan), eight years younger than me, remains. She is loving and warm-hearted and very much a part of our lives.

Gouri, comes from Kerala. Her father, too, was a military officer in the Engineering Corps. Unlike me, however, she knew her family well, including her many cousins. It was Gouri's mother who kept the family bonds strong and made sure Gouri met up at every opportunity with her numerous cousins in Kerala. Some of them, in turn, stayed with us in Rotherham whilst visiting the UK.

Gouri is a retired Consultant Haematologist at Doncaster Royal Infirmary. We have two children: Sonny (Satyajeet) was born in 1977, and Suchi (Suchitra) in 1980.

Sonny graduated with First Class Honours from Cambridge. Because of his knowledge of mathematics and analytical skills, his first post was a good position in the finance-linked sector. He soon began to realise there had to be more to life than pure finance to make large amounts of money. So, with his usual thoroughness, he researched the problem and enrolled with the charity 'Habitat for Humanity'. He then went out to Costa Rica as a volunteer, building homes for impoverished people in tough conditions whilst sharing their accommodation. Helping others became his mission, and at the time of writing, he was the Chief Strategy Officer of Omidyar Network, a philanthropy.

Sonny married Daniella from Lima, Peru. They met as classmates at Harvard Kennedy School of Government, and they currently live in London with their daughter Maia.

Suchi became a Consultant Paediatric Gastroenterologist and is now Chief of the Microbiome Unit at the National Institute of Health (NIH). Interestingly, throughout her Oxford student days, Suchi was familiar with medical research but preferred the practice of medicine rather than an academic/research career. Yet through a twist of fate, her career is developing along her Dad's lines! Her husband Christopher, a physician-scientist, is the Chief of the Laboratory of Myeloid Malignancies at the NIH.

They now live in Bethesda with our grandsons, Daniel and James.

Suchi, by nature, is very much like her mother. Both, in contrast to Sonny's deep analysis, will assess any situation or change by instinct, judging "what's the worst that can happen?" and "can I handle it?". Suchi and her mother are very adventurous in their personal lives, unlike me. I am risk-averse in personal/family matters. In contrast, the research has, on several occasions, been more adventurous, sometimes based on the example of a single patient. This opened up new and unusual avenues, for example, the nature of gut blood flow and the detection of intra-abdominal adhesions.

Mother and Father

Young Chandu & Madhu

Adult Chandu & Madhu

Wedding photo

Our family

Sonny & family

Suchi and family

Far-flung relatives!

During my first major international lecture tour (September 1981), I met physicians, surgeons and gastroenterologists from different parts of the world where the pattern of ulcer and upper gastrointestinal disease varied from that in the UK, an observation which influenced my research many years later!

In Kuala Lumpur, Malaysia, I came to know I had a cousin, Dilip Bardhan, who then filled me in with fascinating details of my family history.

In brief, at the turn of the twentieth century, the British Government looked to improve the colonial healthcare provision in Peninsular Malaya and Singapore. My grandfather, Dr Sarojini Nath Bardhan (SNB), had qualified as a doctor (LMS) from Calcutta Medical College and was appointed in 1907 to the newly established

King Edward VII Medical School in Singapore, where he worked and taught for many years. He was later recruited to set up a pathology laboratory and related diagnostic services in Malacca, having specialised in tropical diseases from the London School of Tropical Diseases in 1921. He had been honoured by the British and Malaysian Governments for his services to the country with the title of Rai Saheb. He passed away in Malacca in 1927.

SNB's firstborn was Pramatha Nath Bardhan, my father. Unfortunately, his mother (my grandmother) died in a cholera epidemic whilst he was still young, so his maternal grandmother raised him in India. At the age of eleven, he was sent back to his father in Malaysia for further education.

Grandfather re-married, and a son, Paresh, my father's half-brother, was born. Sadly, his mother died prematurely, and his father died shortly afterwards. So it was that my father supported his grandmother in India and Paresh's education in Singapore.

On our way to Singapore, Dilip took me to a small house, where a frail elderly man came to meet me. He told me that my grandfather (SNB) had brought him over from Bengal as a fourteen-year-old to work in his laboratory, and he had eventually become the head technician. He then handed me a leather wallet that belonged to my grandfather, giving me this as a gift. I took the wallet. It felt strange, as though the invisible hand of my paternal grandfather had stretched out over time to stroke my head, a common gesture of affection from an elder relative amongst us Bengalis.

The lecture tour proceeded to medical centres on the various islands of East Malaysia, one being the coastal city of Miri, near the border of Brunei, a major oil centre on the island of Borneo. It was here that I met Dr Prabir Sengupta, a surgeon who went on to write a fascinating book on the Bengali families who had moved from East Bengal to settle in Malaysia.[1]

My maternal grandfather, Satyendra Mohan Chaudhuri, was a 'zamindar', a landowner who lived mainly in Sherpur, East Bengal. However, he also had properties in Calcutta in West Bengal and Madhupur in the state of Bihar. He had the interests of his tenants close to his heart and, during the Great Bengal Famine, ensured (by wisely hiding some of the harvests from the authorities who had come to confiscate them) that those who worked for him had three good meals daily. He established a school for the local children and funded their university education. He also established a small maternity hospital for the local population. He was awarded the Rai Bahadur title for his philanthropy. He was a very gifted mathematician and devoted himself to studying.

He had four children with his first wife: one son and three daughters, my mother being the youngest. My grandmother, Binapani Devi, died prematurely from status asthmaticus. He then married Jyotsna, and they had one son, who, in accordance with Bengali custom, had an elaborate name, Satyabrata, but was always referred to by the simpler 'Shelloo'. Uncle Shelloo is the one I knew best amongst my mother's relatives. He, too, was a doctor who served in the Indian Navy and later specialised in Rheumatology.

After partition, the entire family moved to Calcutta by various means, and the grandparents took up their permanent residence in Madhupur[2], their second home, in the state of Bihar.

When my mother was approaching eighteen, plans were put in place to arrange her marriage. Through trusted family contacts, the person chosen was Captain P N Bardhan, a young doctor

---

[1] Malaysia and Bengali Doctors 1907-2012 A Personal Perspective by Dr P R Sengupta
[2] Meaning: '*Madhu*' – honey, '*pur*' - land

commissioned in London into the Royal Army Medical Corps; he had grown up the hard way and so knew first-hand the value of sustained effort to progress. He was more than a decade older, considered 'perfect' in those days.

Father was a tough, independently-minded, towering figure who rose to the rank of Major General and Commandant of the Armed Forces Medical College (AFMC), Pune (formerly Poona), having been Professor of Pathology and the founding Dean of the undergraduate medical college. Mother, in contrast, was gentle and quiet in the background. As was the custom amongst the landed gentry, daughters did not receive formal education but were home-schooled. Mother showed her "inner steel" on father's premature death. Widows were not uncommonly treated as "second class" in India, but she raised Madhu and took her through medical training.

This is a brief account of my ancestral history.

My Father – A Hero Who Made Me What I Am

Our family was small, but it was bounded by love. Father had risen in his career through sheer hard work in dangerous times, having seen military service in North Africa, Palestine, Italy and the Burma Front during World War Two. This included being in Bari when the harbour and the Allied ships were bombed on 2 December 1943, which led to him being severely troubled as many patients in the hospital were lost not only due to poisoning but also some of the wards being hit by bombs. Soon afterwards came the partitioning of the Indian subcontinent; bloody riots and mass slaughter became commonplace.

By the time I was eighteen and a medical student, I had become aware of Father's strong nature and devotion to duty: always helping others, totally incorruptible. By the time he was a colonel and based at AFMC in Pune, transfers became fewer. I could see he was greatly admired by his fellow officers and those in junior ranks, and loved by his medical students. He made everything possible for me by being the perfect role model.

Gouri has been the central pillar in my life, the moral rock of the family, to whom my father often confided how much he loved me. He never lived long enough, however, to actually *say* those words to me. Nevertheless, I regarded him as my guardian angel, reminding me of my moral duty to patients, hard work, determination and discipline, and being upright and aiming high.

Throughout my childhood, he made every possible opportunity for me. One example is when I attended his academic meetings even as a schoolboy. Medicine was above my head, but I loved the discussions and debates, which had increasing relevance when I became a medical student. When I was a schoolboy, he took me to his department, where his technical staff taught me a lot - for example, drawing blood from a chicken. The senior technician was pleasantly surprised that I got it right the first time!

Father was gregarious, and no matter where he was posted, he chose to be with people working in different disciplines - history, philosophy and so forth. He often took me along to their events, which opened a new world of imagination and enquiry.

My father was the single most important person in my early development. Although he worked ceaselessly, he made time for others. After his day's work was done, the people he mixed with were not army personnel. They were mainly teachers, scientists and academicians across a wide range of subjects. He became fluent in French, his proficiency allowing him to serve as an unofficial interpreter! He assisted several charities and helped a school for blind children at my mother's request. We belong to a Hindu family; nevertheless, my father got involved in helping the Catholic Church, in part because we happened to live close to one in Pune. He was awarded the Benemerenti Medal by Pope Paul VI in recognition of his services. In my youth, I felt these activities were highly commendable, and it never ceases to amaze me, even now, how much he accomplished in a hard life cut short at the age of sixty.

At the time, it was exceptionally rare for Indian doctors to be made a Fellow of The Royal College, all the more so for military officers. He commented once that it was a senior British officer who had heard his talk, had a private discussion with him about the work and then, without letting Father know, made the recommendation to the Royal College: he was duly awarded the Fellowship.

This would have been near-impossible without such a recommendation – all the more so as Father's rising career was based on his own hard work, discipline and talent as opposed to nepotism or political connection, which sadly then characterised life in India.

When Father was posted in New Delhi, he introduced me to the senior scientist at The India Meteorological Department, who acted as supervisor for my school project. He was surprised by my interest and was glad to have me in his laboratory, where I spent several days. For the first time, I realised that weather balloons are fitted with sensing devices and a transmitter that sends signals to the ground station. On one visit, I was surprised to see one of the technicians become concerned as signals from a balloon had suddenly stopped. I was familiar with my own experiments at school going wrong, but from this incident, I learnt that such problems also occur in advanced centres!

At night I worked on my essay. My supervisor was pleased by my efforts and helped me to edit it. The title of my paper was 'Radiosonde Flight', which I submitted to the Physics Department. The work won a prize, and I was given the privilege of presenting the project to the older boys of the school's Science Society. Such 'premature' opportunities became a feature of my life, including becoming a consultant physician at Rotherham.

My father was posted back to Pune in 1956/57, and by that time, my class of twenty-five boys was reduced to six, and we were busy preparing for our Senior Cambridge examinations (the equivalent of 'A' Levels). Five wanted to be engineers and so focused on physics and maths. My career choice was medicine, so I concentrated on biological sciences, namely, botany and zoology.

Father knew several people at the Spicer Agricultural College, and he introduced me to the Professor, who was intrigued by my keenness to learn in greater depth and generously reciprocated. I could now begin to really understand the magic of photosynthesis and how plant leaves are organised to maximise this process. For example, leaf pairs on a stem are arranged at right angles to the ones above and below. Such a 'decussate' arrangement ensures that all leaves are exposed to sunlight.

The Professor introduced me to his Research Fellow, who was working on plant chromosomes. For the first time, I could see real chromosomes under the microscope, an image I shall not forget.

I was with the Professor one afternoon when a college clerk came to see him with regard to attending a meeting. His demeanour changed from peaceful to agitated, and he almost shouted to no one in particular, "This place is committee-mad, not work-mad!" I did not understand the details but remembered the occasion as it was to become a feature of hospital bureaucracy!

A major project at the Agricultural College was the breeding of different strains of watermelon. Shortly before four o'clock in the afternoon, stalls would be set up just outside the College gates. Workers returning home by foot or cycle were invited to help themselves to as many watermelon slices as they wanted – the only requirement being that these had to be consumed immediately and the seeds spat out into special bins. The passers-by went away happy, and the College staff now had a large supply of various seeds for their experimental work! I did not know the term then, but I realised this was a very good example of 'lateral thinking' for the benefit of all! I was to see this again and again in my adult life as a doctor.

Uncle Shelloo was very close to my parents. He told my father that he was being very hard on me. Father, of course, intended it for my benefit. My uncle once told me that I had exceeded Father's achievements. However, I take a very different view, best expressed by T Booker Washington, descended from slaves: "*Success is to be measured not so much by the position that one has reached in life as by the obstacles which he has overcome.*"

Mother's love for Madhu and me was boundless but quiet and gentle. Father always regarded Mother as his equal, but in my young eyes, he was a towering figure, so much so that I shamefully took Mother and her love for granted and could not recall openly expressing my love. By the time I resolved to put matters right, it was too late, as she had suffered a devastating stroke which robbed her of speech and mobility. She lived with Madhu in Northampton. On my next visit, I hugged and kissed her and told her of my deep love. She understood, smiled, and we both had tears.

It took maturity to recognise that my sometimes seemingly difficult relationship with Father was mainly in my own mind and my dwelling on imagined slights. It was my Father who made everything possible for me through the gift of a boarding school education at great emotional and financial sacrifice for the family.

When I was at the Radcliffe Infirmary, Father was by then the Commandant of the AFMC in Pune. He would write letters of encouragement, which I found uplifting as supervision was sparse. He was a great Anglophile and told me that the senior staff were survivors of World War Two and of the difficult times thereafter. It was, therefore, necessary to be resilient and self-sufficient. This I endeavoured to be.

In what proved to be my last letter to him, I wrote that my changed approach had borne fruit and a successful end was in sight. In the letter I received from Father in early 1966, he wrote with various pieces of advice, as well as how much he loved me; this was the very first time he had expressed such feelings. It is to him that I dedicated my DPhil thesis. He died suddenly at his office on 12 August 1966.

A prayer of mine whilst at Oxford and in later years was for a chance to meet him, touch his feet (a Hindu sign of respect for elders), and to hug him and say, perhaps for the first time in my life, "I love you Baba (Bengali word for father); *you* have made everything possible."

A final thought. Father was tested by hardship when young and tempered by action in World War Two. He brings to mind Rudyard

Kipling's 'If'. The whole of the poem applies to him, but I am particularly struck by the following excerpt:

"If you can force your heart and nerve and sinew

To serve your turn long after they are gone,

And so hold on when there is nothing in you

Except the Will which says to them: 'Hold on!'"

The Telegram

On the morning of 12 August 1966, I was at the Radcliffe Infirmary carrying out my research studies in the Nuffield Department of Medicine. A secretary from our department located me in the Cardiology Laboratory in the Regius Professor of Medicine's Department, where I was 'locked up' in a whole body plethysmograph, a chamber like a transparent coffin!

The device was a 'state of the art' system to assess blood flow and its distribution after various stimuli. At the Cardiology Registrar's request, I volunteered to undergo studies with nitrous oxide, more commonly known as 'laughing gas'. Nitrous oxide has remarkable effects, striking euphoria and pain reduction in particular; hence it is used today in the delivery suite and at endoscopy. The gas also causes rapid dilatation of the arteries and veins. There is a fixed amount of blood, of course, in circulation. When vessels are dilated, blood flow slows down, and the heart beats faster to compensate. A stethoscope-like device had been placed over my heart and connected to a loudspeaker. After inhaling the gas, I could hear my heartbeat accelerating rapidly, and at one point, a heart murmur developed, much to my surprise. The Cardiology Registrar, somewhat alarmed, asked his Consultant to assess me urgently. He, in turn, concluded the murmur was 'functional', often heard when the circulation is forced to speed up. What a relief!

At the end of the studies, I stepped out of the plethysmograph feeling 'groggy'. The secretary handed me a telegram from India. I cannot recall its precise wording, but it was along the lines, 'Sadly, Major General Bardhan died suddenly at his office this morning'. My father's well-intentioned secretary had sent the message on his own initiative using the contacts list in his keeping. My mother was unaware that I, and many others, had been thus informed; she had intended to tell me later in a kinder way.

Research Fellows at Oxford were each registered to a specific college. Mine was Jesus College, but I lived in a small annexe separated from the main building by a narrow road. This was convenient as I could come and go depending on my research demands at the Radcliffe Infirmary. Inexplicably, a couple of days earlier, I had felt the urge to take down my suitcase from the loft and pack it with my summer clothes and passport. This was to prove providential as it made it much easier to finalise my return to India. To this day, my actions remain a mystery!

My father was much admired by his staff, and I was to learn later from Mother and Madhu that he was adored by his students, who would not uncommonly come home with very little notice to celebrate, usually after having passed examinations!

Military officers retired compulsorily at age fifty-eight, but very senior ones could extend their stay by a further two years. Father, a dynamic man, was appalled at the thought of retiring, so he took on a new challenge as Director of The Central Leprosy Research Institute at Chingleput, thirty-nine miles southwest of Madras (now Chennai).

At the time, Madhu was an undergraduate student at Stella Maris College in Madras. She was in the classroom when one of the nuns called her out and informed her that her father was ill. Madhu later learnt that he had already died, but the nun wanted to soften the blow. She advised Madhu to return home to be with Mother at Chingleput. I flew out from London to Madras on 14 August, too late for the funeral. It was the very first time I had been on a flight. There to receive me was my Mother, Madhu, a staff member and the driver. To our delight and surprise, Gouri and her mother, Mrs. Kumar, joined us for a short period.

Our Hindu customs require that funerals must take place before the next sunset. Alerted by the telegram, Gouri and several students and staff from Vellore set off early that morning to cover the sixty-nine mile journey in the hospital-van for the funeral being held in the afternoon at the cremation ground close to the house. A large number of staff from the Institute attended, as did representatives of the Army. The priest conducting the funeral was from Tamil Nadu, and so was familiar with local Hindu rituals. As Bengali rituals are slightly different, one of Gouri's classmates, a close friend familiar with our customs, was able to advise the priest.

A bugler sounded 'The Last Post'.

On the day after the funeral, Mother and Madhu collected Father's ashes. Hindus customarily scatter ashes in major rivers or the sea, so they travelled to Mahabalipuram, about twenty to thirty miles outside Madras, and cast the ashes in the sea near the submerged temples, a UNESCO world heritage site.

Mother and I returned to our home in Pune for the thirteenth-day ceremony, which customarily marks the end of mourning and the return to normal life. It was also to settle family matters, and I arranged for my sister's transfer from Madras to Pune to continue her studies at Ferguson College. There were also many other regulatory issues to resolve.

Mother and I reminisced. I remember my mother telling me the days shared with Father at Chingleput had been very special. It was like their early married days, full of hope.

I returned to Oxford rather gloomily on the Lloyd Triestino Line ship, The Michaelangelo. The College steward and his sister were very kind to me, both before I left for India and on my return.

Besides filial love, I greatly admired Father, an extraordinary man and my guiding star. Until then, I had been able to control my emotions, but on stepping out early in the morning to walk to the Radcliffe Infirmary, I was suddenly racked by violent sobs.

Mother passed away in the UK on 12 July 2013. Madhu travelled back to India to cast mother's ashes at the same spot as our father's. By sheer coincidence, it happened to be Saturday, 13 August, the anniversary of the immersion of Father's ashes.

Early Life: Adventures & Misadventures

I was born on 16 August 1940 in Jhansi, in the state of Uttar Pradesh, a military base my father had been posted to. Soon after, he was sent to the North African theatre of World War Two. My mother was only nineteen and lacked the security of her wider family, so she moved to Sherpur, the family home. They got to know that partition of the country was imminent and that serious problems were likely to follow, so they moved to Calcutta, where my maternal grandfather had a home.

World War Two raged, and the Kidderpore Docks in Calcutta were repeatedly attacked by invading Japanese aircraft. As a result, it was safer to return to Sherpur, which at the time was in Bengal. After partition, Sherpur fell within the area renamed East Pakistan, whilst Calcutta remained within West Bengal (India).

On the trip, the train halted a safe distance away from Calcutta during an air raid. The window was open because it was hot, and somehow I had managed to crawl through it and fall to the ground. My mother was horrified by my disappearance. The guard found me by the tracks shortly before the train restarted. This was the first of my several scrapes!

A few years later, the family was in Sherpur. There was a large pond close to the house. I remember once I was playing with my cousin, Nandu, several years older, and she fell into the water. Almost as a reflex, I jumped in to rescue her, even though I could not swim! Fortunately, the gardener rescued Nandu, but there was no trace of me – until he stepped on something hard. I was told he reached down and pulled up the 'hard' object – which happened to be my head!

Rescue from a near-drowning

During half-term at boarding school, we were taken to a lake divided by walkways. I noticed a small whirlpool and, out of curiosity, dipped my foot into it. Suddenly, I was pulled down by a strong force and could not get my leg free. My head was close to the surface but kept bobbing in and out of the water. A kindly fisherman waded up and dragged out my trapped leg, which had been sucked into a large pipe. It was a terrifying experience, made worse by visions of drowning. It turned out that I was not the first person the fisherman had rescued! The prolonged pulling by my classmates had caused a large bruise to develop behind my knee. I wrote to my father about this experience, and he told me the swelling was a haematoma, a collection of blood in the tissues. This was the first time I had ever heard of this word – but not the last!

Accident on a train

I was returning from boarding school to my home in Pune during the school holidays. I was asleep on the top bunk bed when the train suddenly came to a stop, and I fell out and banged my head. Within a day, a large painful bump developed and steadily grew bigger. My father asked his orthopaedic colleague for help. The haematoma had developed into an abscess but worryingly, beneath it was a skull fracture. By this time, my eye had closed completely. He drained the abscess, and I started to improve. Father asked me how I could tell the abscess was smaller. I replied, "Baba, I can now see other objects in the room without having to move my head." He congratulated me later for having made a good observation!

Little did I know that such hair-raising escapades were to be a characteristic of my future life!

Doon School (1951-1958)

Doon School

Doon School is in Dehra Dun, Northern India, nestled at the foothills of the Himalayas. The school was modelled on Winchester College.

In August 1951, I was one of the twenty-five new boarders accommodated in the 'Holding House', a single dormitory on the ground floor. Being from military families, several of my classmates and I shared the common experience of our fathers being frequently transferred and education being interrupted. Boarding school gave us some continuity.

A year later, we were divided between the four schoolhouses; the rooms were distributed over two floors, each accommodating six lads. I was assigned to Tata House (named after its benefactor), whose motto was 'True as steel'.

It was only much later in life that I realised the educational benefits Doon School gave me, particularly for the sciences, which

I enjoyed. Such facilities and opportunities came at a price. The salaries of junior and middle-ranking military officers and other central government servants were low, so parents had to sacrifice a lot to put their sons through school. This was a point my mother used to make repeatedly when she could see I was getting 'emotionally separated' from my parents.

A striking feature was the school's encouragement to undertake projects in any field whilst on holiday and to discuss the work on return with our schoolmasters. The school library had a wide range of books and magazines, and quite by chance, I came across a science article on 'cosmic rays' which interested me. So I began to study this in some depth and came across a big textbook titled 'Classical and Modern Physics', which I was allowed to borrow for the holidays.

As an aside, my father was intrigued by the physics textbook, and we often discussed various matters. So grew my attraction towards science books and undertaking experimental work.

The biology lessons were interesting, so I started to collect butterflies and kept them in a ventilated round sweet jar, complete with leaves. From this, my friends and I could observe the laying of eggs, the development of larvae, the formation of pupae, and the emergence of new butterflies. Digging up earthworms was also fun, as was dropping one down someone's shirt on occasions! Its peculiar movement was fascinating and, years later, gave insights into how guts move.

Doon School also introduced me to organised physical training and a range of sports. Earlier I had very little opportunity, but at the school, I began to play the three major sports: football (the term 'soccer' had not yet appeared), hockey, and cricket. Suffice it to say, my school report stated I was "more enthusiastic than effective!" I agree. My father, on his rare visits to the school during term time, saw me playing football as a centre-forward and rightly told me that

I was not doing sufficient to lead the team. Hockey left its legacy; when tackling a chap from the left, his stick swing-through cut my left upper lip, damaged a nerve, and left me with a permanent lop-sided grin. Cricket was interesting, and I began to get the hang of it. Fielding at gully and standing fairly close to the batsman, I dropped some fast catches, after which the coach commented something about the "ancient mariner" who would "catch one in three". I had no idea what he was talking about! However, I was able to hold on to some very good catches in the slips.

There was also an opportunity to indulge in amateur boxing, which was handy! But I slowly realised I was better as an individual player, and this found fruition in swimming and squash. During medical school holidays, I would go to a military club where I could swim and play squash. In addition, I would attend the 'United Barbell Club' in the city centre. So grew my fascination for the gym, which continued when I was a consultant.

Being away from my parents created an 'emotional gap', resulting in a lack of interest in my ancestry. This contrasts sharply with my sister, Madhu, who revered our Father and Mother. She lived with them until leaving for St John's Medical College in Bangalore, returning to the final family home in Pune during the holidays. Even after the death of Father in 1966, she and Mother lived together in India and later in the UK.

School Holidays

Calcutta

I was back from Doon School during the summer holidays, so Father took Mother, Madhu, and me for a short holiday to Calcutta so that Mother could meet up with her relatives.

While there, Father took me to Puri, an Eastern coastal city in Orissa, where his maternal grandmother lived in an 'ashram' (a religious community) for women. We booked into a hotel on the coast and took a taxi to the ashram. My great-grandmother was bent over with age but still active, and she wore a simple white sari, as was the custom for widows. I touched her feet, a sign of respect. She was delighted to see me for the first time ever. Some years later, Father was almost tearful when telling me she had passed away as he felt his only connection with the past had gone. Not having witnessed death before, I did not know what to say or do but instinctively hugged him.

In the evening, we returned to the hotel in a cycle rickshaw. My father got into a conversation with the young rickshaw driver. He was a schoolboy whose father had passed away a year or two before, forcing him to stop his studies and take up his present occupation; his earnings supported his mother and enabled his younger siblings to get through school. Father reminded me that this was the sort of person to emulate, someone who really understood the call of duty and would sacrifice all to support those dependent on him.

I recollect this event years later, for my heart goes out to those who strive to do their very best.

Kasauli and Ranikhet

These are popular hill stations where many spend their summer holidays. We had hired a small house overlooking the hills in Ranikhet. Uncle Shelloo, Mother's favourite brother, was with us, recuperating from an unexplained pleural effusion.

My father had identified a peach farm several miles away, so he expected me to visit, introduce myself, and write about growing peaches for my school holiday project. He made a contact and then left it to me to take it further. I was hesitant, wondering what grownups would think of a schoolboy visiting them for the purpose of doing a project. I finally plucked up the courage and went to the farm. The staff were pleasantly surprised and went out of their way to help. I got so enthused that I visited several times, causing my mother some concern!

The staff showed me different types of peaches, highlighting their appearance, their classification and their appearance under the microscope. They kindly gave me some illustrations and a few fruits, and on getting back home, I took out the stones and pinned them with string to firm cardboard, making them easier to display.

When back at school, I handed in my project, and the biology teacher was pleased with the effort made. These projects taught me a great deal.

The Kasauli trip was memorable for various reasons. We had taken a gramophone with us so that we could share the music with our neighbours. One of the ladies told us that she loved dancing. She was a military psychologist, and she shared her experiences with Father. He was a true polymath; a pathologist by profession, he somehow got involved with psychology and psychiatry and became editor of a journal devoted to this field!

On holiday we were expected to make our own cooking arrangements. A couple of young men from Kasauli came to help with the cooking. So after a long time, Mother was free to go walking in the afternoons, accompanied by Shelloo.

There was an amateur dramatic society which put on dance and musical shows.

There was even a cinema where we saw some films, including one featuring Sabu. Even to my gullible young self, it seemed obvious that this was trying to project the American image, stressing that with American help, roads could be made through the jungles at high speed.

'Collecting clouds in Ranikhet'

Ranikhet is in the state of Himachal Pradesh, at an elevation of 1800 metres. At such an elevation, it was common for the houses to be enveloped in mist and cloud, creating a slightly blurred view on the front veranda. Out of curiosity, I wanted to collect a sample, so I took an empty bottle and faced the open end outwards. Father suggested filling the bottle with water first, pouring it out gently, thus creating space for the mist to enter the bottle.

When it was time for us to return home to New Delhi, the two brothers who had been preparing our meals came to see us off. Mother was a fine cook, but they had taught her some new techniques. They had grown fond of us and were tearful as we said our goodbyes. They touched Mother's feet and bowed to Father, showing great respect. As my father had already told me, good people are to be found everywhere, whether highly educated or otherwise, and such people should always be cherished.

Learning British History

My twice-yearly school report stated that my grasp of British history was appalling. My father demanded an explanation. I replied that the teacher, an Englishman, was nice enough in other ways but hopeless at teaching history. This infuriated my father as an army officer; my protest was tantamount to insubordination. I was summoned to the headmaster's office. He was genuinely puzzled by the contrast between my poor scores in history, mediocre ones for English, and yet high marks in physics, chemistry and biology.

I struggled to learn British history, as did five other fellow students. Having failed our exams, we were ordered to report to the classroom one evening at eight o'clock for the first of several remedial lessons. As we entered the room, the charismatic teacher was writing various words on the blackboard, filling four columns, seemingly unaware that we were there. We looked at each other, wondering what the teacher was doing. He whipped around, jabbing the chalk at me and asked me to choose a word from the list. I vaguely recall selecting 'warfare', perhaps because I could not understand the reason for the various wars within Britain or their wars in Europe. He pointed to the other boys in turn and asked them to choose a word. He continued by saying that if any of these words had caught our eye or triggered a thought, we would love history.

He asked us to think about why such events had occurred, whether it was necessary and was there was any alternative. He asked that we consider what might have happened if a different choice had been made. Nobody had given us this remarkable insight before.

By good fortune, the Shakespeareana touring company, headed by Geoffrey Kendal (father of Felicity Kendal), was staging various dramas at several schools in India, including mine. To see the great works of Shakespeare and others, such as George Bernard Shaw, as the live drama was riveting, and even I began to enjoy the romance of it all. The bonus was that my scores in English improved!

From then on, I remained fascinated by history, which became increasingly relevant for me in medicine, particularly so in my own field of gastroenterology.

I experienced this first-hand at The Radcliffe Infirmary during my research studies as we had to demonstrate an understanding of the history of our subject. I gradually learnt that so-called 'facts' commonly turn out to be more shaded and sometimes even incorrect. Discussions in medicine and in science are commonly peppered with phrases such as 'as is well known'; on deeper enquiry, what is 'well known' turns out to be anything but! This was certainly true in my research area of pernicious anaemia whilst at Oxford. It also proved to be true in Rotherham as our work on peptic ulcers developed, spanning almost twenty years.

For years it was widely believed that Dr Karl Schwarz, Chief Surgeon at Agram (the modern Zagreb in Croatia), was the person who made the clear and unmistakable link between ulcers and acid. His paper was published when diagnostic radiology was in its infancy! It was only many years later that the barium meal examination became the standard diagnostic method until it was superseded in my own generation by gastroscopy.

Schwarz presumably had access to detecting acid, for example, by a litmus test. It is almost at the very end of the paper that he comments, in passing, that acid tends to be present when there is an ulcer. Ever since that time, the entire direction of treating peptic ulcers by dietary, medical and surgical means, and for a while even by irradiation, was aimed at reducing acid secretion. Earlier, operations had involved cutting away a part of the stomach, drastic but necessary. Surgery gradually moved towards selectively severing the stomach nerves controlling acid production.

It was only many years later that a new and radically different approach was developed. The microbe, *Helicobacter pylori*, was recognised as the major causative factor in the development of ulcers, duodenal in particular. This ushered a further revolution in medical treatment as it often cured ulcer disease. For this major breakthrough, two Australian doctors based in Perth won the Nobel Prize: Robin Warren, a pathologist, and Barry Marshall, a clinician.

Less known, however, is that acid plays a key role in infection; the microbe shelters in its alkaline 'pod', snuggles under the stomach's inner surface layer of mucus, 'hijacks' the controls and forces the stomach to secrete even more acid, thereby killing off competition from other microbes for space and food; much indeed like animals and the human race!

Since that single remedial class, my scores in English improved – but I still need help! I developed a deep love of history, which to this day, I find fascinating.

Work Ethics

Priests have come into my life at different times, some by accident and others when I have asked for their advice on matters of medical ethics.

One occasion was different. At Doon School, a visiting American priest made a statement that struck a chord and continues to influence my life even now.

The priest was Reverend Bob Richards. For reasons unknown to me, he gave a talk at our school. The event was held in 'The Rose Bowl', an open-air amphitheatre with the stage at the bottom and the stone seats rising in semicircles to the top.

Reverend Richards was brisk, energetic and spoke forcefully. He had been described, he said, as he introduced himself, as the deacon trying to reach Heaven on his own power, a most apt description of an Olympic athlete who had been a champion pole-vaulter!

"Lord, give me hard work – and plenty of it" was his daily prayer and one which has stayed in my mind ever since. Initially, I was puzzled, for even back then, people strived to acquire labour-saving devices as their economic circumstances improved. When I became a consultant, I had the privilege of slowly building up a wonderful team, and the importance of these powerful and prophetic words really began to sink in.

I took Reverend Richards' words to imply that if our performance is good today, can we make it better tomorrow? In effect, might we strive continually to improve, possibly to the exclusion of all else?

For me, however, the mantra of ceaseless striving to improve was always counterproductive. Gouri pleaded with me to make "us time" in my diary, an opportunity to be with each other and perhaps go to a cinema or play. I did not manage to do this because the sustained efforts on behalf of our patients began to bear fruit. Our first PhD project broke new ground by differentiating the circadian rhythm of acid secretion by the stomach in healthy volunteers in striking contrast to patients with duodenal ulcers.[3] From then on, research expanded, leading to several more PhDs, MDs and Masters Degrees and to publications and presentations at national and international gastroenterology events, unusual for a district general hospital.

Reverend Richards was ordained as a minister in the Church of the Brethren in 1946. Famously he asked one of the church attendees, a young Billie Jean King, what she would do with her life. She replied that she was going to be the best tennis player in the world, which of course, she achieved.

I would love to have been able to let Reverend Richards know how his speech given over sixty years ago, had influenced my life.

---

[3] Continuous 24 hour ambulatory monitoring of intragastric pH in man. BK Kapur, PJ Howlett, NG Kenyon, MJ Lunt, JG Mills, RH Smallwood, AJ Wilson, KD Bardhan. *Clin Phys Physiol Meas* 1987; 8:123-32

Six Early Life Lessons

I learnt much from my teachers' aphorisms. Some of these are memorable, and I can still recall them decades later. The following six examples came from my medical school teachers, who, by coincidence, all were American.

1: The nature of expertise

During my early clinical years and internship, I met an American anaesthetist on the College bus taking the medical students to the hospital. A conversation developed on the nature of expertise. He commented:

> "The Novice knows he does not know, hence strives to gain experience and expertise.
>
> The Expert knows how to do it, when to do it and does it very well.
>
> The Master knows how to do it when to do it, does it very well – but also knows when *not* to!"

His comments had a lifelong influence: I was to learn that my enthusiasm to help ('intervene') exceeds my judgement! I cannot explain how one single meeting with a stranger on a short bus journey could have had such a profound effect on my professional life and, in the process, of making me a 'better doctor', I would like to think.

Two examples illustrate this.

The first is feeding by percutaneous endoscopic gastrostomy (PEG).

PEG feeding is very useful, but it is crucial to know when not to do it. When a patient is beyond curative help, it is kinder to withdraw treatment and to concentrate on palliation, always, however, with the consent of the patient and their family.

As a result of our experiences, I became much more 'selective' about which patient ought to undergo PEG tube placement. In effect, I followed the wise advice given many years ago.

Thankfully, as our team's standard practice, we had developed reviewing outcomes. This showed that against expectation, cancer and stroke patients fared far better than the elderly who did not want to eat.

The second example concerns cardiopulmonary resuscitation (CPR).

My DPhil research work was mainly laboratory-based and involved working long hours, both day and night, in The Nuffield Department of Medicine based at the old Radcliffe Infirmary at Oxford. As I was already in the hospital, I volunteered to join the CPR team as I was well-placed to answer the crash call. As a result, I gained much experience! Some very senior doctors of the hospital staff chided me gently, "Chandu, you have to learn when intervention serves little purpose".

Many years later, the 'Do Not Resuscitate' (DNR) policy was introduced, a crucial element of which was that the patient's consultant must make the decision. We now have a professional CPR team, better placed to know when to intervene and, importantly, when not to.

Such examples have drawn me towards 'mysticism' and 'fate' (meditation and inner reflection). Senior colleagues and trainees have often teased me for such leanings, as I am supposed to be a man of science! Nevertheless, I continue with meditation as, with advancing age, I have learnt there is more to medicine than 'hard science' alone.

2: Give a person a break

A consultant paediatrician at Christian Medical College Hospital (CMCH) told me shortly before I left for Oxford that some people are denied opportunities in life, so if ever I was in a position to help, I should try to do so.

As a young man, he had wanted to become a doctor, but his plans were interrupted when the USA joined the allies in World War Two. He had been attached to an engineering unit where he was given various opportunities, 'breaks' indeed, that had served him well.

I, too, had unexpected opportunities. One striking example during my training days at Sheffield was being allowed to work with my endoscopy mentor, and this had far-reaching beneficial consequences. I learnt a great deal from him, not only medical science but also the art of mentorship, which I have applied to the many trainees who have worked with me.

In turn, I was eventually able to give young doctors and scientists opportunities through The Bardhan Research & Education Trust (BRET), a family charity we devised with an independent chairman and trustees. The accomplishments of the BRET-supported people and of our other young trainees have given me joy far greater than anything I have done, and I am immensely proud of them.

3: Improvise

My year's internship in 1963 ended with three months of training in obstetrics and gynaecology (O&G), which I opted to undertake at a mission hospital in Ranipet, about thirty miles away from my medical school. The Medical Director widened the scope of my work from O&G to include taking care of all the women admitted, irrespective of their problems! One of my classmates was instructed to take care of all the men, irrespective of their problems. In practical terms, however, there were often times when we inevitably 'crossed over'.

I learnt about the importance of 'improvisation' from the consultant surgeon in charge, who somehow sensed my 'eccentric' nature long before I did!

A patient was admitted with a fractured leg that required traction but, unlike at the medical school, the necessary equipment was unavailable so I was asked to improvise. I was puzzled when I was asked to look through the window and comment on what I saw. I saw nothing but grass and sand, and that is when I thought of the solution to the problem!

I borrowed a shovel from the portering staff, filled a jute bag with sand, placed it in a larger bag and double-tied it in case the sand contained tetanus spores, potentially hazardous on a surgical ward even when wounds were covered. We connected the now-heavy bag over the patient's bedrail, thus providing traction. Our patient recovered, a satisfying result.

On several occasions later in my life, I have had to improvise to make things possible.

4: Chandu, let's find out for ourselves before jumping to conclusions

This advice came from a consultant orthopaedic surgeon at Vellore. The year of internship at CMCH comprised three-month periods in medicine, surgery, public health and obstetrics/gynaecology. Within surgery, the interns spent a month in the orthopaedic department.

On several occasions, I noticed that some patients who had X-rays taken would suddenly disappear without seeing the specialists! I learned later from the department's porters that the patients had gone to Puttur to see 'the bonesetters'. Until that moment, I had not heard of Puttur, and, in my immaturity, I was outraged that these people had gone to see 'quacks' instead of 'proper' specialists. Many people, including several senior doctors, shared my views based on stories of complications patients suffered after having been to Puttur. A particular problem was deformities of the forearms and hands after sustaining a fracture around the elbow when they ended up by seeing the hospital specialists.

One of our senior American surgeons wanted to know much more about the bonesetters before drawing conclusions. Vellore to Puttur and back, approximately sixty-five miles, would take almost three hours each way, an entire day I thought would be wasted, but our surgeon accepted the price in search of information. So several of us in the department joined him and travelled in the hospital van to Puttur.

We reached Puttur, and people pointed out where the bonesetters worked. To my surprise, I saw people lying on the ground on stretchers or standing with crutches, the line extending for at least a hundred yards to an open-air hut where the bonesetters worked.

I was fascinated! The bonesetters were gentle, kind and honest, their deeds speaking volumes. Crucially, their patients trusted them. If they felt surgery was required, the bonesetters would advise accordingly. With their permission, our surgeon examined several patients and commented to us juniors that he could not have improved upon their treatment. He added that a tertiary centre could do no better, even after carrying out many expensive investigations.

We learnt that the bonesetters were members of the same family, and their skills were passed down through the generations. The family was well-to-do as they had land available to grow rice. Being so blessed, they felt it their moral duty to help others, and so developed their art. They did not charge anything except for bandages and splints, the latter fashioned out of bamboo, which was plentiful in southern India and cost very little.

When there was an injury, but no fracture, one of the remedies they used was to massage the area with a soothing ointment. In others, more force might be required, so the bonesetters, supporting themselves on wooden rails, stood on the affected area and massaged using their feet.

We set off back to Vellore late in the afternoon, and soon darkness set in. The journey gave me time to reflect, and I felt thoroughly ashamed of myself; I had gone to mock, if inwardly, but returned humbled. The following week we discussed the events we had witnessed. Earlier I mentioned seeing patients who had suffered permanent damage to their forearms and hands after having been to Puttur, the implication being that the bonesetters were irresponsible. This proved to be totally wrong as the damage was caused by the patients' delay in reaching them.

I learned two major lessons from the trip. First, do *not* rush to judgement! Unless there is something criminal or morally reprehensible, wait, and assess the situation; ask what might be missing; time and a fuller picture can resolve many problems.

The second is that chaps like me, steeped in science-led medicine as students, at times put our newly gained information above true knowledge and wisdom. Patients may not have had as much formal education as us, but they possess enormous life experience, often of greater value.

I honestly believe I learnt from this incident and took it to heart; it has improved me as a doctor.

5: 'You've got to learn when to button your lip!'

This advice was given when I got into an argument with an American nursing matron. It took me back to an incident in Year 2 at Vellore when we were doing pre-clinical studies at the College campus.

There were twenty-five in my class, roughly equal numbers of men and women, and we were given the opportunity to visit the hospital to see our future workplace. There we met the formidable Professor of Cardiology. She asked me to tell her the normal heart rate, and when I replied it was between sixty to eighty beats per minute, as I had learnt in Physiology, she insisted that it was seventy-two. I persisted in arguing. She was very annoyed and reported me to the Principal.

The following day I was summoned by the Principal as my conduct had placed him in a difficult position. He pointed out that although I was correct, it would have been diplomatic and polite to remain quiet.

'Buttoning my lip' became an issue at the Finals examination held in Madras, the State capital, to which all medical schools in Tamil Nadu were affiliated. I was astonished that my scores were the highest across all medical schools. The exception, however, was in Public Health. This disappointed me as I loved this subject. It was exciting going to distant villages and dealing with people with varied problems without immediate access to the facilities of CMCH.

My father, though pleased with my performance in Medicine, Surgery and O&G, questioned the poorer outcome in Public Health. I stated that I had argued with the examiner as he was wrong. My father commented that there is a time when it is best to stay silent.

6: Chandu, you don't have all the answers

As I was preparing for the interview in New Delhi for the Rhodes scholarship, I was advised that I would not always have all the answers. The long train journey gave me time to reflect on this advice, as well as that given by several others.

During the interview, I was asked various questions: some I could reply to confidently, but others I could not, and I admitted this without any hesitation. Several candidates attended, and two of us were selected.

There have been several instances in my subsequent career where staying silent got things done more effectively than by argument!

Vellore

Christian Medical College

I had decided that medicine would be the career to pursue, so after Doon School, I noted that Christian Medical College (CMC) in Vellore had an all-India admission policy. Having heard about this renowned medical school started by Dr Ida S Scudder, I was keen to train there. Dr Scudder was an American medical missionary whose family had served in India for many years. She was appalled to witness women dying during childbirth, as the families were too orthodox to allow male physicians to treat women. This made her train as a physician, and she returned to India to train local women to become doctors. The motto she adopted was 'Not to be ministered unto, but to Minister', and this was the ethos of the training at CMC.

By the time I joined, men were also being admitted to what had started off as a women-only medical school. CMC was located in Vellore, eighty-five miles west of Madras (Chennai).

At the time, the selection process started with a multiple-choice examination paper open to candidates from all over India. Then a hundred candidates were selected for an interview at CMC. We were given several tasks, some individually and some in groups. The group tasks were to assess whether we were individualists or team players. This whittled down the numbers, and fifty were finally selected – equal numbers of men and women. Out of these selected fifty, there were only a handful of non–mission sponsored candidates whose education was supported by their parents, and I was very fortunate to have been selected in this group. I joined the 1957/58 batch of CMC.

The training at Vellore allowed the ordinary to come together to achieve extraordinary results. Over the years, I came to realise that our training was second to none. We had access to such a huge number of people requiring medical care that we had a wealth of clinical experience.

Our alma mater had an international reputation, so it was common to have distinguished doctors and scientists visiting CMC. We had some very specialised units, especially for tropical sprue. I began to get a glimpse of how research in science works. In particular, I enjoyed the chance to discuss specific points with our consultants, made easier by the fact that most lived on the college or hospital campus.

As all the students lived on the campus, we were a close-knit community, and it was at the men's hostel that I formed lifelong friendships. We have kept in touch and visited our close friends in different parts of the world and have enjoyed having them in our own home in Rotherham.

A few of my friends and I enjoyed playing pranks, and one particular incident which comes to mind is of when I got the idea of playing a crazy trick on my classmate. Each of us had a single room. During the hot summer nights, we tended to keep our windows wide open. During the year when we did Anatomy, each of us had been given a skeleton to dismantle to study individual bones. I took the skull, put a lighted candle within, and placed it on the windowsill from the outside of my friend's room. I then gently prodded him awake with the end of a stick! The first thing he saw was the glowing skull, and his screams awoke the rest of the hostel! My friends and I were rolling on the ground with laughter.

I was very fortunate to have received awards in most medical school subjects, along with the medal for the best outgoing student of my year. To my surprise, I had the honour of obtaining the top rank at Madras University when I passed my final exams.

During the years at CMC, I was privileged to have been taught by many outstanding physicians who were inspiring human beings along with being leaders in their field. One of these was Professor Edward Gault, whom I would like to mention in more detail.

Professor Gault was one of the most memorable people I have ever met. I learnt a great deal from him; he influenced my life in many ways, and I remain eternally grateful.

An Australian descended from a long line of missionaries, he was the Professor of Pathology. He trained as a surgeon but felt his results were not as good as he had hoped and that others could do better. So, he changed direction and retrained as a pathologist. Today, an audit is considered standard practice but this was not so when I was a medical student. Such humility, combined with his sustained efforts to help people, created a huge impression which has remained throughout my medical career.

Training in pathology started in Year 3, along with the clinical subjects of medicine, surgery, obstetrics and gynaecology, and rural medicine. Included in the pathology module was time devoted to 'clinical pathology', where we examined blood, urine and faeces.

Training in pathology was very well organised. It started with an hour's lecture (including discussions), followed by a short break. Then our class of twenty-five students was divided so that half would proceed to examine pathology specimens stored in jars, explanatory details displayed on boards. The other half would examine tissue slides under the microscope, again aided by explanatory boards. The two groups would then switch over. At the end of the afternoon, we would gather once more for a general discussion.

My father was then the Professor of Pathology at the AFMC in Pune, and he would meet Prof Gault at regional and national conferences. After one such occasion, Prof Gault asked me to see him during a lunch break. He then relayed my father's 'complaint' that I did not keep in touch with the family. I promised I would write a letter that night, but he said he had a couple of sheets of paper and wanted me to write the letter while he prepared tea, and we shared his sandwiches. I was surprised and touched, and carried out his instructions. I did not have any money for postage, but he asked me not to worry about this as he had the necessary stamps.

I was always keen to learn new things, even if not directly related to our training. One day he asked me to see him at his office to let me know that a British expert was visiting from The London School of Tropical Medicine and Hygiene to investigate mosquito-borne illness. The expert kept the insects in several small cages wrapped with muslin. To feed them with blood, he would simply loosen the muslin and stick his finger in, from which they had a blood meal. I was amazed by his ingenuity! It was only many years later when in the UK, I learnt the phrase 'lateral thinking'.

I was not the only one impressed by this great man. At his farewell, a large number of medical students and doctors came to see him and his wife, Edna, also a doctor.

Prof and Mrs Gault returned to Australia and settled down in Melbourne. The following is an extract from a special article.[4]

He began work (1962-68) for the RACS, providing courses and advice (particularly in pathology) to postgraduate students, initiated a registry of soft tissue tumours, and curated a museum for the college. In 1969-73, he held a part-time appointment as a senior demonstrator in pathology at the Austin Hospital, Heidelberg; he was later commissioned with Alan Lucas to write its centennial history - A Century of Compassion (1982).

I had been invited to give a series of talks at major centres in Australia on our expanding research work on the treatment of duodenal ulcers. My hosts kindly altered the itinerary to allow me to meet Prof and Mrs Gault.

It was a sad sight: Prof Gault was in bed, almost skeletal and unable to recognise people. His wife was by his side, explaining he had undergone prostate surgery, had experienced serious complications and suffered brain damage. It was so sad to see him reduced to this state.

---

[4] Gault, Edward Woodall (Ted) (1903–1982) by Suzanne Parry. Australian Dictionary of Biography. Vol 17 (MUP) 2007

'Bring up the Bodies'

In mid-1963, during my rotating internship year, I was urgently summoned to the Medical Superintendent's office. Feeling very apprehensive, I entered his office. He was holding a document in his hand, which he began to wave around as he asked me why a death certificate had been completed, but no one of the name on the certificate was in the mortuary.

My heart sank as I felt I would be held responsible for this 'mystery', which he would regard as one of my pranks carried over from my student days! But gradually, we resolved the matter, and I was 'cleared'.

The patient in question was a young woman with advanced tuberculosis (TB) of the abdomen, affecting both the gut and the peritoneum. TB causes gut ulcers and scarring, which thickens the peritoneum, choking off its blood supply. The poor lady had the look of imminent death: sunken eyes, barely conscious and breathing in short gasps. She had already been categorised as terminally ill; nevertheless, intravenous lines were attached, more 'symbolic' than effective.

The senior house officer, two years my senior, was utterly exhausted after dealing with the poor lady through much of the night, displaying the call of duty that characterised our training. The end was imminent, so she had signed the death certificate before going off duty the following evening.

Meanwhile, the registrar, a couple of grades higher, a lovely and helpful chap, came to the ward to assess another of our patients. Seeing the dying lady and judging there was nothing to lose, he injected a high dose of hydrocortisone through the intravenous lines. This provided a life-giving boost, and she improved slightly but passed away the next morning. The ward orderly, however, had already delivered the death certificate to the Superintendent's office, hence the confusion!

The second episode was in the Medical Ward at Montagu Hospital in 1978. I was at home in my study when a young doctor telephoned me late one night, incoherent with panic. I had to ask him to calm down before telling me what had happened. Distressed, he told me the patient in the side room had passed away. It was unclear why he was so troubled as this was an expected death, of which the patients' relatives were aware. He informed me that the relatives had been waiting outside, and when they entered the room, the patient woke up, causing a great deal of upset and confusion. Barely able to suppress my laughter, I asked him not to worry. The patient passed away about half an hour later. The incident caused much merriment amongst the young doctor's medical and nursing colleagues, and for a while, he was nicknamed 'Lazarus'!

A Christmas Gift

These events occurred in a small mission hospital in Ranipet, about forty miles from The Christian Medical College. Tragedy struck ten days before Christmas in 1963, its cause unknown and unfamiliar even to senior medical staff, let alone to raw recruits like me.

A young woman was brought in by car: she was dehydrated by diarrhoea, and her eyes were sunken and rolled up with the whites showing, the typical look of imminent death. Her veins were collapsed but I managed to get a needle in at the elbow and rushed in the saline but to no avail: she soon died.

The second patient, a young man, was brought in a bullock cart in similar circumstances but perhaps not as far-gone. Despite rapidly infusing saline, he, too, died three or four hours later. A young child was brought in shortly afterwards but died before we could do anything.

A senior nurse raised the possibility of cholera, but this seemed improbable as that area of southern India was well away from the zones of cholera epidemics. Despite the unlikelihood, I decided in some desperation to examine the patients' faeces to search for any evidence of cholera. The two technicians who staffed the tiny pathology laboratory told me this was an area where medics had hardly ever set foot – until I arrived! The technicians were bemused but helped me set up a 'hanging drop suspension', a technique I had learnt earlier.

A special microscope slide with a shallow well at its centre is used. A minute drop of the liquid faeces is placed on the *under* surface of a coverslip, which is then placed over the well, allowing the drop to hang. At high magnification, I was able to see the curved rod-shaped organisms swimming, propelling themselves with hair-like filaments at one end: imagine them as a banana being propelled by a hairy tail! The appearance was typical of a class of organisms called vibrios, of which the cholera organism is but one. In these dreadful circumstances, it became clear that cholera was the most likely cause of the illness.

Many more patients were admitted, and most of them died. The stocks of saline had run dangerously low, so I phoned the head pharmacist at my teaching hospital for help. Unfortunately, he could not spare the large amount of saline we needed or make up any more by early next morning, our deadline. He knew me and my habits but was astonished by my suggestion that my mates and I would travel over that night to make the saline solution under his guidance! Along with a senior doctor, we got into the hospital mini-van and the driver, fired by our urgency, raced with us to the teaching hospital, hoping desperately that the ageing vehicle would not break down. We arrived at about ten o'clock. Guided by the head pharmacist and his technicians, we prepared many litres of intravenous saline and hoped it would last us for the next two to three days. The head pharmacist and technicians were alarmed to see bits floating in the solution but agreed there was no time for perfection! I tried to comfort him by requesting that he regard the floating bits as 'snowflakes', bearing in mind that Christmas was approaching!

We arrived back at the mission hospital as dawn broke. Meanwhile, many more patients had been admitted, most of whom were desperately ill. Despite administering large amounts of intravenous saline, several died. Then, against all expectations, one survived, then two and then a third. From about three days before Christmas, every patient survived.

Though eternally grateful, I could not help but wonder why so many had died earlier. The answer gradually emerged years later.

The cholera organism secretes a toxin which forces the cells lining the gut to pour out fluid, resulting in diarrhoea. The entire lining of the small gut, however, renews itself over four or five days, being replaced by new cells uncontaminated by the toxin. Survival grows by the day, so if the victim can be kept alive by rehydration, the disease clears by itself.

Tired by lack of sleep, we were nevertheless euphoric that the cholera mini-epidemic had cleared.

Age and experience give us a chance to reflect. I had missed the deeper significance of that Christmas more than half a century ago; namely, it is not 'I' but the '*we together*' which allows the 'ordinary' to achieve the 'extraordinary'. This is particularly striking in a crisis, as events that Christmas showed when so many showered us with kindness and goodwill.

A truly wonderful Christmas gift.

Thirst – Yet Fearing Water

A couple brought their fretful son to the clinic, the most striking feature being his thirst. He was in his father's arms, and when his mother offered him a drink, he would dip his finger in it, lick it and scream in absolute fear.

I was aware of rabies and of a particular type named 'hydrophobia', the absolute fear of water. I had also heard from others of instances where they would show the child a picture of a dog, and the youngster would recoil and shriek: unethical perhaps, but those were different times.

The consultant, a gentle middle-aged man, explained the situation and the dreadful prognosis to the parents. The father, over six feet tall, unusual in South India, started to sob violently. The mother was virtually immobile, in a state of shock. There was no treatment available, so they took the child back to their home. There was no further information, and presumably, the child passed away.

This incident affected me profoundly as it was a desperate human situation, which words alone cannot describe; even more so given that so much had happened in such a short space of time. I learnt a great deal about medicine, humanity and grief.

The Descent of Man

During my three months of surgical internship in 1963, one month was devoted to orthopaedics.

Like most others, the orthopaedic ward had a modified Nightingale design - a large rectangular room with the space divided into four rows, housing about 40 beds. The nurses' station was at the centre with a row of beds on either side.

At the far end of the ward was a small space with tables and chairs where doctors could write their notes or have discussions: this was out of sight to anyone entering the ward.

A patient had been admitted after damaging his leg following a fall. His face seemed familiar – and he turned out to be the ward orderly (porter). My knowledge of Tamil, the local language, was poor, so before examining him, I asked an interpreter what had happened. The patient seemed evasive as he said it was an accident. Ultimately, the full story emerged.

I felt sorry for him yet was relieved, as the consequences could have been much worse, if not fatal. With an appalling lapse of my bedside manner, I started to smirk as the interpreter translated, but the neighbouring patients, all local people, had no such inhibition and laughed loudly. The story spread rapidly, and the ward was soon in a hilarious uproar!

The hospital is in the centre of the town, and the students' hostel, my home for five years, was on the college campus, five or six miles away, and linked by a circular route. The college bus would take us to the hospital by one route in the morning and return by the other in the evening, passing by the beautiful "Ooteri" Lake, partially hidden by a grove of palm trees, some bearing coconuts and the others areca nuts. Coconut palms are tall, growing up to a hundred feet, whereas areca palms are much shorter, up to about twenty feet. The sap from the trees was distilled to make liquor.

Vellore is located in Tamil Nadu, where alcohol is prohibited, a law observed more in its breach but difficult to prove as there were no breath testing kits in 1963. The distillers hid the cache of alcohol near the top of the palm trees and would retrieve the required amount for their customers, always men, to drink in comfort. Women *may* have had a 'nip', but I had never come across this – or, more likely, had missed it!

Palm trees have rough bark, with thick, jagged scales jutting out, making climbing up or down difficult. I have seen experts use rope looped around the tree to ascend in short steps: when the loop was level with the climber or just above, he would expertly flick it up higher in a fraction of a second and ascend in short steps. One can picture descent, too, would be hazardous.

The interpreter told me the orderly had inexplicably chosen to get the alcohol for himself – and my admiration for the soon-to-be patient grew! Instead of bringing the alcohol down and drinking it in comfort, he drank it whilst high – literally! In consequence, the descent was swift!

Fortunately, he tumbled as he landed. Matters could have been far worse if he had fallen on his other end, causing concussion or a skull fracture, bleeding and demise.

Thankfully, it ended well, save limping for a few weeks. Our hero had to laugh at his antics and recounted the incident when he came to bid me farewell just before I left for the UK.

Grimace

This striking event occurred at The Christian Medical College Hospital (CMCH) at Vellore in the first half of 1964 when I was a house officer.

I was summoned urgently to see the young lady who had been admitted to our ward. She had recently given birth at home, but this joyful event started to go wrong. Previously outgoing, her mother noticed her daughter's demeanour was now "unusual" as she seemed to be wilfully disregarding her questions, almost ignoring her. By the time she reached the hospital, the picture had advanced: in response to questions the nurse and I asked, her expression changed to something approaching a grin, an involuntary movement. Her mother was understandably alarmed that the joy of her daughter's childbirth was turning into a nightmare.

Two things struck me: her expression and her difficulty in breathing, which would require ventilation if it worsened. Even my chief, an outstanding and very experienced clinician, was puzzled. It finally dawned on me that her expression, the grin in particular, might be an example of 'risus sardonicus', which I was taught resembled a 'smiling cat' – which, even in those early days, I thought was far-fetched! Today's literature, however, emphasises that 'risus sardonicus', also known as a 'rictus grin', is an abnormal sustained spasm of the facial muscles caused by a variety of conditions, including tetanus.

The CMCH was a nationally recognised tertiary centre for cardio-respiratory surgery. Hence, its ventilators were used mainly to support patients undergoing such operations. These ventilators were in short supply. As her ventilation worsened, we approached the respiratory consultant, a charismatic doctor from Birmingham, and he came to the rescue. The Principal of CMC had invited him and his wife (also a doctor) to join the staff, and they remained in India for ten years.

They had been on several mountaineering expeditions in India, conducting respiratory studies on their colleagues at high altitudes. With extraordinary ingenuity, he developed a novel mechanical ventilator that did not require electricity! Instead, the patient's breath triggered the ventilation, a remarkable innovation which, at the time, I sensed did not get the recognition it deserved.

Sadly, the young lady passed away, a disaster.

Today, tetanus immunoglobulin is used for treatment – but I cannot recollect if it was available in 1964. In southern India in the 1960s, people living in rural communities might not have received tetanus vaccination in childhood nor have the facilities for safe childbirth at home: no midwife, no thorough cleaning of hands and so on. The CMCH had a wonderful rural programme which spanned many villages, and I regarded it a special privilege to visit these places to try to help.

The first two years as a medical student covered the study of anatomy and physiology. Respiratory medicine, however, was overshadowed by cardiothoracic surgery; hence, my understanding of the subject was limited. This was rectified by the wonderful lectures the consultants from Birmingham gave in my clinical years (year 3 to year 5), bringing respiratory physiology to life.

This is the first time I learnt about indices such as vital capacity, forced expiratory volume (FEV) and so forth, and could actually see how these measurements were made. Even in those early days, I sensed such indices offered a means of tracking a patient's progress in much the same way as monitoring blood pressure or blood glucose levels.

Their lectures were gripping as they showed images of them carrying out respiratory measurements on colleagues at high altitudes amidst the snow, a masterclass in communication.

Benign Britannia: British Soft Power

British soft power, in my experience, has meant a gentle spirit of friendship, heart-warming kindness from so many, and fruitful collaborations with colleagues in the UK and overseas.

To me, 'soft power' seems easier to 'sense' than to define; several tangible government- and institution-inspired initiatives have profoundly influenced my life.

There was no formal announcement but, late in 1960, during our third year of medical education, we became aware that brand-new British medical textbooks could be obtained at low cost. This seemed very odd but actually proved true! Such books, though readily available in India, were expensive, an added burden on parents funding their children's medical education or on the various missionary groups sponsoring three-quarters of my class of fifty students. These books could now be borrowed for the duration of one's studies at a low annual cost, about one-tenth of the full price. Only several years later, British and American textbooks were re-published in Asia, making them more affordable.

Familiarity with such textbooks gave us basic information from which we gained an understanding of the theory and practice of medicine and its application leading to 'knowledge'. Combined with other British publications, it also gave us something 'intangible', a 'feel' for the British culture of openness, debate and discussion. As a result, I did *not* feel 'uncomfortable' when I arrived at Oxford in October 1964, a young inexperienced medic who had never been out of India. The atmosphere at this great centre of learning has been described as 'rarefied', yet I settled in smoothly!

As an undergraduate, I sensed British textbooks, compared to American ones, were more clinically oriented and rich in description. American textbooks seemed rather 'direct', and investigation-oriented. A good example is the excellent Textbook of Medicine edited by Cecil & Loeb, and later by Prof Paul Beeson. Studying both British and American textbooks gave me a more comfortable rounded view.

The British Council built libraries in many large cities in India, a very visible example of soft power. When home from medical school during holidays, I often visited the one in Pune. In addition to the wide range of books and magazines, several British newspapers were available. Comparing 'The Times' with major Indian newspapers such as 'The Times of India' or 'The Statesman', I could see the same stories reported differently. I had learnt from the teacher who fired my interest in British history that there may be more than one view of an event: the papers at the British Council library confirmed that.

The British Council also sponsored distinguished British scientists and doctors to visit Commonwealth countries to give talks about the latest developments in their field and sometimes to take short sabbaticals working with local staff at an institute or hospital. In early 1964, two visiting professors in haematology and gastroenterology from the internationally renowned Hammersmith Hospital in London spent a few days at Vellore. I was the junior doctor in Medical Unit 2, headed by a gastroenterologist. He invited the gastroenterologist to join us on ward rounds, and I found the professor's comments really illuminating. I happened to mention my impending period in Oxford, and he told me that after finishing my research period, I should spend time with him learning *real* medicine!

In his unit, I learnt a different style of medicine and new technologies. One example, for instance, was the recognition of coeliac disease. The altered appearance under the microscope of the small gut's lining is diagnostic. Taking the biopsy, however, was time-consuming; it involved feeding down into the small intestine a special 'cutting' capsule attached to a long tube. Employing this technique, I later diagnosed several patients at Sheffield and Rotherham with this condition. Today this method has been replaced by simpler means, thankfully!

Another example of British soft power is the role of The Royal College of Physicians of London. They developed the Overseas Doctors Training Scheme (ODTS) to strengthen its links with the Commonwealth. This was led by an eminent gastroenterologist who knew me from the Nuffield Department of Medicine, where he was one of the consultants. The ODTS aimed to select good candidates, based on merit alone, to join an established department in the UK to gain further experience, and required the recipient to know the sponsor personally.

Through ODTS, a young doctor from India joined my unit for three years (1990-93), two as Registrar and the third as Research Fellow. Judging from the publications, he assumed our unit was large but was dismayed to see how small the unit really was! However, he soon learnt it was less the numbers and more how the team worked together, supported by our magnificent patients, which made us productive. Growing in confidence and ability, he proved outstanding, and together we produced novel work.

Oxford

Rhodes House

Following my clinical training, I was surprised to be selected for a Rhodes Scholarship, which brought me to the UK. The subject of my DPhil was 'Studies on Intrinsic Factor in Man', which I completed in 1967.

The Rhodes Scholarship[5] *(taken from the Rhodes House website)*

Established through the Will of Cecil John Rhodes in 1902, the Rhodes Scholarship was a truly visionary project for its time. Over a hundred years later, the Rhodes Scholarships are the oldest and perhaps most prestigious international scholarship programme in the world, enabling outstanding young people from around the world to undertake full-time postgraduate study at the University of

---

[5] https://www.rhodeshouse.ox.ac.uk/scholarships

Oxford (ranked first internationally in the Times Higher Education rankings for 2017 and 2018).

One of the founding aims of the Scholarship was to identify young leaders from around the world who, through the pursuit of education together at Oxford, would forge bonds of mutual understanding and fellowship for the betterment of mankind.

Our reputation as the world's most distinguished academic scholarship rests not on the controversial life of our founder Cecil Rhodes but on the enormous contributions our Scholars have made to the world, and the qualities sought in a Rhodes Scholar - intellectual distinction combined with concern for others, energy to lead, and a focus on public service - remain as compelling as they were over a century ago.

Heading to Oxford in September 1964 was my first time outside of India.

After the initial bouts of seasickness, I settled down to enjoy the voyage. I had time to reflect on what lay ahead. I expected to be away for the scholarship and then return home. I was apprehensive but determined to make the best of the opportunity I had been given.

The journey took ten days – nine on the ship, The Galileo Galilei, belonging to the Lloyd Triestino Line. I set off from Mumbai, with short stopovers at Aden and Messina, disembarking at Genoa. From there, I travelled overnight to Tilbury, central London and then to Oxford.

The Galileo Galilei

As is the custom in Oxford, each student is allocated to a particular College where they reside. I was at Jesus College in the heart of the city, close to the libraries and the science campus. Jesus College was founded in 1571 by a group of Welshmen led by Hugh Price, Treasurer of St. David's Cathedral. It was the first Oxbridge College to be founded after the First Protestant Settlement by Queen Elizabeth I.

As a postgraduate student, I stayed at the annexe on Ship Street. This was very convenient for laboratory work and when I started clinical projects.

Life in the Laboratory in My Early Days

At my boarding school in India, I gained quite a lot of experience working in the laboratory at an elementary level and recognised the importance of being well-supervised and the help technicians can provide.

We gained experience working in the physiology laboratory at medical school during Year 2. In Year 3, we started to learn how to make certain 'simple medicines' – and doubts began to grow. For example, in one class, we prepared 'Blaud's pills', an iron-containing preparation made from ferrous carbonate to treat anaemia. These tablets were black, soft, and looked like goats' droppings, which even the patients were concerned about! The only difference was that the odour of the two was different.

Another experiment was making ointments to apply on bruises, burns and abrasions. Despite our best efforts, the 'ointment' my classmates and I made was rough; we could only imagine it would hurt when applied to a raw wound.

We later learned that some domestic staff who cleaned the laboratories after classes were selling the preparations in the nearby villages!

After finishing medical school, I gained first-hand research experience in the Nuffield Department of Medicine (NDM) at Oxford, headed by a gentle, charming chief. The title of my research work was 'Studies on Intrinsic Factor in Man'. I presumed that in a world-class institution, all the basic work would run smoothly, and it was only at the cutting edge that I would need to develop new techniques and test these, and also that all such explorations would be well supervised.

To my surprise, the reality was different!

The Odour of Nail Varnish Remover!

A feature that struck me in my very early days was a strong odour of nail varnish remover! There was a very sweet, short lady lifting a heavy bottle of acetone onto the laboratory tabletop, and from there, she would try to pour the contents into smaller containers. Unsurprisingly, much would be spilt in the process, hence the strong odour.

A solution suddenly came to mind involving the following steps:

1. Keep the large container on the desktop.
2. Use a flexible plastic tube to carefully suck up some acetone, ensuring I did not get a mouthful. I then lowered the other end into a small container. Once the liquid was connected at both ends, it would flow steadily down, and several containers could be filled without spillage.

Two ladies, both senior technicians, kindly commented, "That's jolly clever". A senior member of the technical staff responsible for ordering various items wondered why he had not thought of such a simple solution. They would tease me by putting on a thick Peter Sellers Indian accent, saying, "You are not as stupid as you look"!

Electrophoresis

One afternoon, I was at the Radcliffe Infirmary canteen when a youngish man sat opposite me. He asked what I did, so I told him of my frustrations with electrophoresis, starch gel in particular (with repeated rupturing of the flasks holding the gel and, on one occasion, an explosion!). He turned out to be a senior scientist who worked in the department of biochemistry at the Oxford Science Park. He was using a new technique of acrylamide gel electrophoresis, something I had never heard of. He kindly asked me to see him at his lab, where he showed me the small, compact, but expensive equipment.

Importantly, parts of the equipment could be 'homemade', using two sandwich boxes, glass tubes and electrodes.

When the Chief retired, he was succeeded by a Yale University professor keen to invigorate the laboratories with new staff and different ways of thinking. Sir Hans Krebs, of Krebs cycle fame, was keen to continue his work after retirement. He was given a fairly large laboratory space connecting the NDM's top floor with the general biochemistry laboratories. Such proximity led to some pleasant exchange of views between Krebs and myself.

Separation: Paper electrophoresis

Nobody seemed to have any definite plan on how best to carry out electrophoresis, the key step to separate proteins in the blood.

One day I met a very pleasant gentleman outside the NDM who asked who I was and what I was doing. He turned out to be a senior figure in the adjacent biochemistry laboratory. I told him about my experience with paper electrophoresis; absolute failure was the only consistent result! He offered to help, kindly took me to his laboratory and asked the technicians to show me how to set things up properly.

For the first time, using horizontal paper electrophoresis, I could see the bands of protein separating. One of the elements I used to measure intrinsic factor (IF) was ^{58}cobalt vitamin B12, a radioactive isotope. I could now measure the distribution of radioactivity along the paper strip. I was so grateful for the gracious help that was given to me.

Separation: A costly 'typo' error

In an attempt to get a clearer separation, I was advised to use vertical paper electrophoresis. The paper strip was folded over a supporting rod, with both ends dipping in the buffer. This almost doubled the length available for proteins to separate. Hence results were more reproducible. I followed the instructions carefully this time, taking advice from other professional biochemists, yet the results were no better. In exasperation, I wrote to the author and asked for guidance. He was very sympathetic and, indeed, very embarrassed. There was a typographical error in his book, and as a result, I was using a very weak buffer, incapable of separating the proteins. He spotted the error, but the publisher declined his request to temporarily insert an 'erratum' notice, preferring to wait until the book was republished!

Thankfully, fortune was to smile on me!

Separation: 'Getting the worm out'

The acrylamide, which has radioactive bands, sticks to the inner walls of the glass tubes. Getting the gel out is not easy, and sometimes it fragments completely. Then a thought struck me: the benefit of doing a lot of clinical medicine! The needles we use for drawing blood are short, but lumbar puncture (LP) needles are long. The ward sister kindly gave me one LP needle to experiment with. I connected its hub to a short rubber hose which, in turn, I attached to the tap in the laboratory sink. I then inserted the needle gently between glass and gel and turned the tap gently. Result: The force of the water made the gel shoot out! It was then a simple matter to dry the gel, put it in a tube and count the radioactivity but maddeningly, the results were not consistent. I checked and re-checked every step – and at one point, even wondered if it was because of the amount of light in the laboratory! But doing electrophoresis in bright daylight versus at night did not make any difference.

Acrylamide gel electrophoresis: Getting consistent results

My supervisor then made a suggestion which transformed everything. The solution with the proteins comprises gastric juice and serum from the patient, each in small amounts only. These are mixed by placing the test tube bottom on a mechanical agitator (vortex mixer) and shaking the contents for thirty seconds. The supervisor suggested I should try shaking it for longer. I was dubious because the lab experts had already told me to follow the instructions to the letter, but I nevertheless complied. Outcome: Consistent results.

Time for hooray! – 'bloody marvellous'. Phew!!

Publications/Reference

1. Simplified technique of immuno-electrophoretic assay of human intrinsic factor on acrylamide gel. KD Bardhan, STE Callender, GH Spray. *Gut* 1966;7:566-8

2. Blocking and binding auto-antibody to intrinsic factor. KD Bardhan, JR Hall, GH Spray, STE Callender. *Lancet* 1968;1:62-4

CPR

At Vellore, I came across 'Pye's Surgical Handicraft', which gave a wide variety of helpful tips to medical students and young doctors. When I started my rotating internship, the first rung of the training ladder, I came across a man who had collapsed in a hospital corridor. I recalled reading about external cardiac massage (ECM), a new concept. Absurd as it may sound, I quickly checked Pye's book, which I kept in my white coat pocket, to ensure I followed the sequence of instructions correctly. Specifically, I checked for the pulse in the neck along the carotid artery and used my stethoscope to listen to the heart. There was neither pulse nor heartbeat, so I started ECM and was surprised and delighted when I could hear heart sounds and feel pulsations in the neck.

A senior staff member saw what I was doing and told me to stop wasting time and to get on with the work he had asked me to do. However, he graciously agreed that the patient now had an audible heartbeat and a pulse, and his circulation was restored for a few moments. Sadly, the gentleman passed away.

The story soon spread that I had been seen reading Pye's book: some senior nurses were astonished that I was "engrossed in my studies at this critical time" – and this was a compliment! Importantly, I could never have foreseen the far-reaching effects this incident was to have in both my professional and personal life.

In those days, defibrillation was used only in patients having cardiothoracic surgery. When the chest was open, defibrillator paddles could be applied directly to the heart. However, the outcome was almost always poor if a patient suffered a cardiac arrest outside of the theatre.

I left Vellore in August 1964 and got ready to go to The Radcliffe Infirmary at Oxford, then to its original site on Woodstock

Road. I started my research at The Nuffield Department of Medicine (NDM), where most of my time was involved in laboratory work concerning intrinsic factors and the absorption of vitamin B12. Periodically, I carried out clinical work, cardiopulmonary resuscitation (CPR) in particular, which, being new, was introduced with a flourish! I often worked in the laboratory late into the night, and as it was adjacent to the medical ward, I could reach patients very quickly.

A special 'crash' trolley had all the necessary equipment readily available, including electrocardiograph (ECG) leads to stick to the chest. Importantly, it was fitted with infusion sets to deliver intravenous (IV) saline, thereby giving an access route for the delivery of other drugs, specifically, sodium bicarbonate, to neutralise lactic acid. As knowledge and experience grew, other drugs were added, in particular two local anaesthetics, Lignocaine and Procaine, which also had anti-arrhythmic properties.

Adrenaline stimulates the heart. For years, the dose was shown as a ratio of 1 in 1000. Common sense finally prevailed, and the dose was stated in milligrams! A further advance was to make the drugs available in single-use preloaded syringes.

Mr John S Stewart, a consultant surgeon, had shown that the build-up of lactic acid reduced the chances of survival. He generously invited me to collaborate. From him, I began to understand both the science of resuscitation and how to succinctly convey the findings and significance to others in plain language.

During cardiac arrest, the pupils start to dilate; they contract again when circulation is re-established. I was uncertain about this, so I sent a letter to the British Medical Journal[6]. Mr Stewart had been invited to lecture elsewhere when someone drew his attention to my letter. He replied that this was an important piece of evidence

---

[6] Dilated pupils in cardiac arrest. *British Medical Journal* 1966;1:484

produced by a young research fellow in another field who had started collaborating with him.

In response to my letter, a doctor from Southampton wrote about a two-year-old girl who had "ingested" thirty grams of quinine sulphate, resulting in convulsions and cardiac arrest. Resuscitation was successful despite the presence of fixed dilated pupils, which did not revert to normal for three weeks. This was presumably due to a direct action of quinine on the eye.

In passing, my father saw this letter and wrote, saying I had not been clear. Father was a wonderful role model and 'critic', in the kindest sense of the word! Looking back at my letter almost fifty-five years later, I fully agree with his criticism as my original letter was 'too wordy'!

Those who had been trained in CPR were issued with a special pager. To summon the crash team, anyone anywhere in the hospital dialled '222', which alerted the switchboard to send out a special signal to the CPR team. The person carrying out ECM would know that the anaesthetist would be alongside very shortly and would take care of the airways by endotracheal suction and ventilate mechanically with an Ambu (Artificial Manual Breathing Unit). This collapsible bag is squeezed to push in air and then suck it out, resembling, in this way, the normal respiratory cycle.

At that time, there was a fashion for mouth-to-mouth ventilation, referred to as 'the kiss of life'. It certainly made good drama in film and TV but was phased out in medical practice as mechanical ventilation was safer. On reflection, this would be true in a hospital, where everything is at hand, but I have, from time to time, asked myself what I would do if someone collapsed in a remote place.

In the early days, success was uncommon, but we persevered nevertheless. As sometimes happens in times of crisis, 'black' humour intruded! One quip circulated told of a senior registrar who was desperately seeking a consultant post at a time when vacancies were few. Summoned by a crash call to attend to a consultant who had collapsed in the toilet, he paused only to check if the consultant was a physician or not!

Out of interest, I would sometimes go to the ward to listen to the heart sounds of patients admitted with a heart attack (myocardial infarction). I listened in particular for a third heart sound, which signified further stress to the heart and possibly indicated a poorer outcome. This distinctive sound, called a 'gallop rhythm', can be mimicked by tapping a table surface with the index, middle and ring fingers. I was listening for this in one patient when, all of a sudden, his heart stopped. I immediately started ECM and asked the nurse to send the crash call. The team arrived and restored sinus rhythm – the normal pattern – but sadly, the patient passed away shortly after.

Humorous incidents also occurred! A nurse called '222' when she saw a flat line on the monitor of a very senior consultant physician admitted with a suspected myocardial infarct. I was in the lab at the time of the crash call, so I rushed into his room and found him sitting up reading a newspaper! He was surprised to see me, saying, "Hello, Chandu. What can I do for you?" I was flustered and blurted, "Sir, I was bleeped because you had a cardiac arrest." "Don't I look good for a dead man?" he quipped. The explanation was simple: the ECG leads had slipped off! The doctor recounted the story to my seniors in the Nuffield Department of Medicine, and many of his associates, causing much hilarity!

I earned the nickname 'Dr 222'! During the Christmas pantomime, where medical students usually impersonated consultants, I was caricatured as a dark chap wearing a short 'dhoti' – similar to a loincloth. A student fitted with a long black moustache and in a Peter Sellars-style heavy Indian accent muttered, "Hey, where is my bloody 222 machine?"! I missed the first performance but attended the next night, where the mirth and laughter were all the more remarkable as I was there in person!

There were two further 'humorous' incidents!

I should make clear that the crash call team would lift the patient off the bed and place them on the floor. ECM demands short sharp pumping, usually five times, with a few seconds gap to allow air to be squeezed in and out of the Ambu bag. If ECM is attempted on a bed, the mattress absorbs much energy, and cardiac output falls.

On one occasion, the patient awoke during resuscitation and told me in a broad Australian accent, "Get off my chest, you silly bugger"!

The other was when my colleagues and I dragged a patient out of his bed, placed him on the floor and started ECM. During one of the pauses for ventilation, he awoke and said, "Can I get back into my bed now?"!

Finally, we had success! Great for the morale of the resuscitation team and other staff. Re-energised, we went on to further successes. During a grand round presentation, I could not help quipping about one 'real life' incident. Ward lights are dimmed at night. A patient was successfully resuscitated, but on seeing a dark chap (me) emerging from the gloom, he mistook me for Mephistopheles (aka the Devil), screamed and promptly collapsed again! The whole place burst into laughter, so much so that I could not assure them that we had resuscitated the gentleman! The next day I had to go to the Radiology Department, and the consultant recounted the incident and said, "You brought the house down, I was told. You really are a character!"

My research involved carrying out gastric secretion studies and taking gastric (stomach) biopsies to correlate the stomach's radiological appearance against the amount of acid and intrinsic factors produced. I learnt that research is not a solo performance but is built gradually upon the help and guidance of many, from junior staff to senior, highly experienced people. The consultant was pleased that I acknowledged his help and that of his colleagues in my DPhil thesis.

My participation in crash calls was greatest when the second Nuffield Professor of Medicine, Paul Beeson, took up the post having earlier been the head of department at Yale University, Connecticut. During the whole time I was at Radcliffe Infirmary, I noticed that there were several Americans, usually in senior positions. On Professor Beeson's arrival, many more joined, including some who were keen to work with the resuscitation team. I had been at small seminars attended by Professor Beeson when I had had to dash off to attend crash calls. He was pleasantly surprised, I was told, by the sheer energy and dedication with which we worked.

The development of CPR permeated many departments. The Professor of Neurosurgery was amazed by this new development, particularly when my colleagues and I rushed in whilst he was operating! He recounted the event on many occasions, I was told.

Those working towards a DPhil from Oxford (PhD at other universities) are required to show an understanding of the history of their subject, and I learnt a lot from this. Belatedly, I searched for literature concerning the development of CPR by using ECM, from which we identified a report referring to William Kouwenhoven, James Jude and Guy Knickerbocker.

CPR: From Oxford to Rotherham

I started at Rotherham full of hope and energy. I wished to specialise in gastroenterology, but, as mentioned elsewhere, most physicians in those days were regarded as 'general physicians'. They only later were allowed to express interest in a specific area. Having had reasonable CPR experience at Oxford and recognising its value, I was keen to develop it at Rotherham. I planned to discuss the subject with the nurses in the medical ward in the morning and to repeat this for the night shift. After that, I wanted to repeat the process on the surgical wards.

Being young and naïve, I did not realise my good intentions might not always be viewed this way! The ward nurses were ambivalent: they understood my intentions were good, but this "bee in my bonnet", as one put it, was causing problems, not least disrupting the staff's working pattern. The senior nursing officer was upset and phoned to "tick me off"; his actions were supported by the chief nursing officer. My profuse apologies were graciously accepted. Indeed, they gave strong support and brought about the involvement of my senior physician colleagues.

The philosophy of CPR gradually spread; today, we have a full and truly professional team in charge. All doctors have mandatory training. A rota of staff was established so there would be no gap in the service.

Crucially, data is gathered continuously and analysed, for as experience has shown, the pattern of 'crash calls' and their outcome has gradually changed. For example, recognising in-patients 'at high risk' and taking preventive measures has reduced the need to summon emergency help. This is similar to "a stitch in time" or regular car maintenance to reduce the need for rescuing from "breakdowns".

CPR: The downside

As CPR spread, I started to hear 'negative' comments, such as intensive care doctors tend to be more intense than caring!

With experience and maturity, I realised that death is not a failure in those terminally ill, and it would be wrong to attempt resuscitation. The decision not to resuscitate is a major one, and thankfully today is made by a consultant instead of junior staff, as was once common. Today we have hospices for 'end of life care', where comfort and dignity are paramount.

It is essential to realise that we cannot always save patients' lives with CPR. I would like to mention two patients.

Frozen alive

10th February 1967, Radcliffe Infirmary at Oxford

The distinctive crash call '222' bleep sounded at 8.00 a.m., summoning the cardiopulmonary resuscitation (CPR) team members to the Casualty Department. A forty-two-year-old lady had been found unconscious, half-immersed in a canal, with a syringe and a bottle of intravenous Pentobarbitone (a short-acting sedative) by her side. Breathing in gasps, her pulse was weak and soon disappeared. Her appearance was striking, something I had never seen: she was pink down to her scarlet legs; she had a cold trunk, small pupils, and an absence of 'capillary refill', a sign that peripheral circulation was impaired.[7]

The Lecturer in Anaesthetics and one of the housemen joined me. I was the 'odd man out', researching full-time in pernicious anaemia but interested in cardiac arrest and CPR, and had been a team member for some months.

---

[7] Capillary refill: If one presses the skin or nail in the healthy individual, the area underneath blanches but the colour returns as soon as pressure is removed.

We put the patient on her back on a hard board and commenced CPR. I started cardiac massage whilst a tube was placed through her mouth into the trachea and began to ventilate her manually with a special bellows-like bag. Meanwhile, the houseman placed a needle into an arm vein, commendable as the veins were collapsed. He infused sodium bicarbonate to counteract the build-up of lactic acid, which occurs when circulation fails. The electrocardiogram (ECG) showed ventricular fibrillation, a condition in which the heart muscle fibres contract chaotically and so cannot drive circulation. A low-reading thermometer was placed in the gullet, which runs close to the heart and reflects core body temperature. It was only twenty-two degrees centigrade, indicating severe hypothermia, the normal being around thirty-seven degrees. Survival rates at such low temperatures are poor, even amongst the fittest.

Defibrillation paddles were quickly placed on the patient's chest to deliver an electric shock to 'kick-start' the heart back to a normal rhythm. This was unsuccessful, as were further shocks given in short succession, even though the acidosis had been corrected. So, we wrapped her in four electric blankets, but the core temperature was still low at twenty-four degrees centigrade and only slightly better an hour later. Her pupils began dilating, indicating that the brain was starved of oxygen.

On the spur of the moment, I suggested we ask the heart surgeon to warm her blood in the heart-lung machine. He had just arrived to start his ward rounds and thought the suggestion "crazy – but interesting", and kindly agreed!

In those days, heart surgery was done mainly to fit artificial valves. This required the heart to be still, with the circulation maintained by the heart-lung machine, the device which removes blood from the body, passes it through an oxygenator and returns it. Crucially, it would allow our patient's blood to be warmed up. Setting up the system takes many precious minutes, unaffordable as every second of interrupted cardiac massage would reduce her already-low chance of survival. Large bore tubes were inserted into the femoral artery and vein at the groin and guided into the heart. One tube was placed in the right atrium. It is located at the top of the heart and receives venous blood, its oxygen content low, the gas having been extracted by the tissues. Another tube was introduced into the left ventricle, which receives blood oxygenated by the lungs, from where it is pumped out into the general circulation.

The patient's temperature began to rise slowly. The heart stirred a flicker of activity, then the occasional contraction, punctuated by 'false starts' when it reverted to a chaotic pattern requiring further defibrillation. Finally, stable circulation was established, and we could discontinue cardiac massage after three and a half hours, which we sensed must be some sort of record!

The patient recovered slowly, enduring many setbacks on the way, which was unsurprising - when the circulation is poor for long periods, most of the body's systems are inevitably damaged. The outcome, however, was gratifying, and she was eventually able to return home.

Hypothermia is a common emergency in civilian and military life, so we wanted to place our experience on record to help others. Journals devoted to anaesthesia or cardiac surgery were 'super-specialist', so we decided to submit our account to *The Lancet*[8], which has a very wide readership. Being popular, it seemed highly unlikely it could spare precious space on a single patient, even if unique. Fortune smiled on us, however, as the editor must have felt it was worth it!

Experience has taught me that novel ideas sometimes emerge during a crisis, when a patient's survival is at stake and decisions

---

[8] Severe hypothermia as a result of barbiturate overdose complicated by cardiac arrest. RH Fell, AJ Gunning, KD Bardhan, DR Triger. *Lancet* 1968;1:392-4

have to be made rapidly. Such circumstances can allow everyone to contribute, from the most junior to senior doctor present.

In day-to-day medicine, however, a wider range of staff can join in: nurses, dietitians and, importantly, the clerical and other support teams. When I became a consultant some years later, I maintained such an approach and was rewarded by being able to lead a very good team from whom I always learnt much.

Frozen heart

In 1969, I was a registrar at the Royal Hospital in Sheffield. I was urgently summoned to the Casualty to see a young man found unconscious and hypothermic in his car in the Peak District. He was a tall, muscular trainee surgeon who, having failed his Final FRCS examination, decided to end his life and took an overdose of a sedative. Recalling the incident at Oxford, I contacted the cardiothoracic surgeon at Northern General Hospital and asked if he would consider warming the doctor's blood on the cardiopulmonary bypass system. The blood was warmed outside the body, and the normal temperature was restored.

The heart showed signs of activity but could not beat fully as ice crystals had developed within the muscle fibres, the only time I had witnessed such an event. I felt very sorry for the doctor, a young life blighted, but was full of admiration for the consultant, who kept an open mind and accepted a suggestion from me, a trainee.

As mentioned earlier, CPR has influenced my professional and personal life. I have had multiple cardiac interventions, including two coronary artery bypass operations. I also had a cardiac arrest, from which I was resuscitated by my team as we were on-call!

I owe my life, very literally, to our hospital's resuscitation team, and it is to them that I would like to dedicate this section on CPR. Thank you, and God bless you all.

Sheffield

After completing the DPhil in 1968, I returned to clinical medicine, spending three months in neurology at The Churchill Hospital in Oxford and six months in gastroenterology at The Hammersmith Hospital in London. From there, I moved to the Royal Hospital at Sheffield in February 1969 to continue working in medicine as a Medical Registrar. The intention was to spend eight months each with different consultants, but before I could complete this, the Professor of Medicine told me to apply for the lecturer's post in his department.

I became a lecturer in the professorial department in May 1970. The professor was an authority on influenza, and his research laboratory in this field was at the Lodge Moor Hospital some miles away. He also had a laboratory at The Royal Hospital, where I carried out some experimental studies. Importantly, he held a very high position within the University Grants Committee for medical schools. Though distinguished, he was known for his short temper!

On one occasion, a patient was admitted who was not responding to the antibiotics the professor had started him on. I could not contact the professor so discussed it with one of the senior lecturers interested in respiratory medicine, and he recommended that I change the antibiotic. On his return, the professor was furious and gave me a severe scolding in his office, and this could be heard in the laboratory. He banned me from the wards, insisting I ask the pre-registration houseman for permission to see the patients I was looking after!

The other senior lecturer, Dr Gwen Barer, rushed over, took me to her office and made me some tea. She added that my boss was known as the 'smiling tiger' and that I must not lose heart as several others before me had suffered a similar fate. To have someone to turn to who understood and was sympathetic was truly wonderful.

I was introduced to Dr Barer in 1969 when I came up from the Hammersmith Hospital to Sheffield to be interviewed for the two-year rotating Registrar post. She was very kind and asked me to let her know the outcome of the interview. She congratulated me on the appointment, and I met with her again shortly after taking up my post. She and her husband, the Professor of Anatomy at Sheffield, lived at Fulwood, close to where I shared a flat with a couple of friends.

Knowing I would be on my own at Christmas, Mrs Barer kindly invited me to their home, where I met their three sons. She would have many guests, and it was fascinating to listen to their discussions, for example, literature from Soviet Russia by Alexander Solzhenitsyn and others. I was introduced to the game of 'Go', in which opponents seek to gain ground, a different approach to that used in chess.

When we returned to Rotherham after Gouri and I got married, Mrs Barer invited us to lunch. This was the first of several meetings, and she soon became a dear family friend.

Mrs Barer loved to help junior doctors from overseas, particularly those from Eastern Europe, and I met several at their home.

Mrs Barer passed away peacefully in November 2006. A most remarkable person: a scientist and investigator of note, she always wanted to help people, particularly newcomers. Gouri and I loved her, as did many others.

Bitter Almonds

Among the many patients I saw at Sheffield, one patient left a lasting impression.

There was a pungent odour of bitter almonds as I approached the unconscious patient, and it was quite overwhelming when I stood next to him. It was strange that my friend and colleague Dr Barrie Hillman did not even notice the unusual odour.

We were both in the Professorial Medical Unit at The Royal Hospital in Sheffield: Barrie was the registrar, and I was the lecturer. Our team was on duty for medical emergencies when Barrie took an urgent phone call one evening from a GP. A patient accidentally swallowed cyanide, collapsed shortly afterwards, and struggled to breathe.

It turned out that none of the Casualty Department staff on duty had ever dealt with cyanide poisoning. So Barrie and I began preparing ourselves in the time available during the patient's ambulance journey. We hurried to the library and rapidly checked the drugs formulary and textbooks for current views on management. The head of the Casualty Department then drew our attention to a new antidote, Kelocyanor, which had just been added to the emergency drugs held in the department.

The 68-year-old patient had no circulation and was not breathing, yet he was bright pink. These contradictory appearances were strongly suggestive of cyanide poisoning, the sort of rare 'small print' stuff which often sticks in medical minds!

The electrocardiogram (ECG) showed the heart was contracting, though clearly to no effect, as there was no pulse. We started resuscitation: external cardiac massage, manual ventilation using a bellows-like device, and intravenous alkali to counteract the build-up of acid. None of these measures had any discernible effect. So, for the first time at the Royal Hospital, we used intravenous Kelocyanor. Amazingly the pulse returned promptly; indeed, it raced away, and the blood pressure rose. Spontaneous breathing, however, did not return even after further Kelocyanor.

Rational doctors would concentrate on resuscitating the patient. But my 'maverick' nature got the better of me; we began to collect blood samples, to the surprise of the other staff, who probably felt this was no time for 'academic curiosity'!

In desperation, we washed out his stomach with a variety of chemicals and started mechanical ventilation. Shortly afterwards, he began to breathe, and within minutes his breathing raced away. Our joy was short-lived, however, as the improvement soon faded. Back to square one, we gave more intravenous antidote and resumed ventilation, this time with a machine.

Some hours later, he began to pass dark stools, indicative of bleeding from within the digestive tract. After more antidote, it soon became clear that the poor man had irreversible brain damage. The heart finally stopped, and he was pronounced dead almost forty-eight hours after the accidental poisoning.

At autopsy, there was widespread damage. The heart was baggy with bleeding on its surface. The lungs were flooded with fluid in certain parts and collapsed in others. There was extensive bleeding into the stomach lining. The dark stools had developed as a result of bleeding from a couple of dead areas in the small gut. The brain looked 'angry': swollen and red. Its lowermost parts, the pons and medulla, were black, the equivalent of gangrene. These two structures contain the crucial centres regulating circulation and breathing. Little wonder the patient did not survive despite the huge doses of antidote and all our other measures.

Not only had we measured blood levels of cyanide whilst he was alive, but we also did the same for samples taken at autopsy: bile, urine and brain. I arranged for these measurements simply out of curiosity, little realising that such data were unique at the time.

Cyanide poisoning: a wider perspective

We learnt that cyanide was used widely in the manufacturing industry, but poisoning in the workplace was rare because of the stringent UK safety laws. Poisonings, when they did occur, were usually by inhalation, rare even then, almost half a century ago. Poisoning from swallowing cyanide was rarer still.

A touch of science

Oxygen from the air we breathe has to undergo a complex chain of events before the body can use it. This chain is blocked by cyanide. With the circulation at a standstill, oxygen in the blood and tissues stays trapped. That is why victims of cyanide poisoning have a striking pink appearance.

Many treatments for such poisoning have been tried, but each carries significant disadvantages. However, clinicians are forced to take the risk when the situation is desperate. Kelocyanor (dicobalt edetate) is a cobalt-based compound. Cobalt compounds are effective antidotes to cyanide but are toxic in themselves. 'Chelation' is a chemical process which removes the toxic properties of many metals, including cobalt. Many such chelated cobalt compounds have been developed, but back then, dicobalt edetate, almost fifty years ago, was the best.

In cyanide inhalation, the victim can be removed from the contaminated zone. However, when poisons are swallowed, they continue to be absorbed. Washing out the stomach prevents further absorption. In our patient, we took the additional precaution of placing antidote in the stomach to prevent, or at least reduce, the amount of cyanide absorbed.

The Inquest

Until proven otherwise, the Coroner necessarily had to take the view that the cyanide poisoning may not have been an accident. However, the details that emerged left no doubt that the tragedy was accidental. The patient had gone to visit his brother, a keen gardener. On these visits, they would often sit in the garden shed, where his brother kept a supply of alcohol. But this time, the patient poured himself a drink whilst waiting for his brother to join him. Unfortunately, the whisky bottle he selected was one his brother had used to store weed killer.

Despite their sadness, the family were very kind and thanked us for our efforts. We were deeply touched and humbled.

A Clinical Postscript: Another patient

We later admitted another patient who, because of the nature of his work, had access to sodium cyanide. He had swallowed a small amount and collapsed shortly afterwards but remained conscious. We injected three lots of Kelocyanor intravenously over a few hours, but alarmingly, he developed abnormalities of heart rhythm, felt very sick and began to vomit. On discontinuing the antidote, he improved. Curiously, about thirty-six hours later, he developed a red rash on his chest and arms, which started to fade the next day. We presumed this was a side effect of Kelocyanor, which until then had never been described.

Another touch of science: Nature's evolutionary arms race!

On exploring the subject further, Barrie and I were surprised to learn that cyanide is present in bitter almonds and many other plants and fruits, such as apples, peaches, apricots, lima beans, barley, sorghum, flaxseed and bamboo shoots!

Plants store an *inactive* form of cyanide in their cells. The enzyme, the specific chemical that unlocks the inactive form, is stored in a different compartment. When an insect nibbles, the compartments are crushed: the chemicals mix and cyanide is released. However, when an herbivore chews, many more compartments are crushed together, releasing far larger amounts of cyanide.

This process has been likened to breaking a glow stick to mix the chemicals that make the stick fluoresce. This is referred to as the "cyanide booby trap".

A final postscript – on a happier note!

These events took place in 1971, but the paper was not published until March 1974.[9] Publishing in medicine and science commonly takes a long time as even if considered favourably, a paper may require extensive revision several times before it is finally accepted.

Barrie moved to general practice in 1972, but we lived fairly close to each other and met regularly at home. One day, we reflected on the matter of our paper and assumed it must have been rejected. Nevertheless, we plucked up the courage and got in touch with the editorial team. To our astonishment, we learnt that the paper had been accepted, but owing to a mix-up, they had forgotten to inform us!

---

[9] The use of dicobalt-edetate (Kelocyanor) in cyanide poisoning. B Hillman, KD Bardhan, JTB Bain. *Postgraduate Medical Journal* 1974;50:171-4

The Driving Test

While I was in Sheffield, I shared a flat with two other lads, slightly younger than me. The bus stop was very close to the flat, so I would take a bus early in the morning to the hospital and reverse the process in the evening, sometimes very late.

My flatmates and others at the hospital advised me to take the driving test, purchase a second-hand car, and become independent.

I recognised their point of view but felt that the drawbacks exceeded the benefits; there was very little parking space at the flat and almost none at the hospital. As I often spent twelve to sixteen hours at work, I had limited opportunities to use my independence. The situation suddenly changed when I moved to Bradway, about seven miles away, with my friend Roger Penny, who had purchased a flat.

I had passed my driving test in Pune before enrolling in medical school. I knew I would have to pass the UK driving test if I wanted to drive here. Even though we drive on the left side of the road as in the UK, driving in India is very different as there are many types of vehicles, as well as animals, going at different speeds on the road, and the use of the horn usually clears a path ahead! Driving rules are there to be ignored.

I enrolled at a driving school. The instructor was a bit surprised at my driving style and asked if the car I used in India had only three gears! I told him the car was a Hillman Imp and had four gears. On another occasion, he ticked me off as I was "making his toes curl"! Eventually, however, I became more comfortable and took the driving test.

I passed the test, but the examiner asked if I was trying to impress him by stopping at the crossroads and looking both ways exaggeratedly. I was told to do so by my instructor, was my reply.

I eventually purchased a second-hand Hillman Imp, which my colleagues at the hospital would refer to by its distinctive colour, Saluki bronze.

Some months later, I became a lecturer in the Professor of Medicine's unit. There was much banter between the two students and myself, partly because of the teaching I provided, which they greatly appreciated, and the free hand I gave them when it came to experimental work. They insisted I had passed my driving test only because of good luck and that the examiner had taken pity on me. They demanded that I pass the Institute of Advanced Motorists (IAM) test to prove I could drive!

I got to know, quite by chance, that the police at Sheffield West Bar Station provided advanced motoring lessons. They gave four evening sessions, each of about two hours, with a brief interval for tea, coffee and biscuits, all free of charge! At the end of the final evening, we were introduced to IAM holders who would train us for the examination. A date for a test run was set, and several of us turned up.

I was told that reversing safely was a key requirement. So I inserted bamboo sticks in plant pots and practised reversing between these. People in the other flats were initially puzzled by my antics but encouraged me. Finally, I went on long drives with my flatmate and his fiancée.

I got the IAM manual and practised it over and over again. I then really began to appreciate how helpful the manual was. For example, to look out for exhaust pipe emissions as a sign that a car might pull out. Similarly, it instructed the reader to be wary of a ball on the road as a child might run across the road to retrieve it.

The day of the test dawned, and many at the Royal Hospital genuinely wished me good luck.

The examiner instructed me to take him on a specific long and winding route approaching the Ladybower dam and back. He would suddenly ask questions to test for alertness and anticipation. At the end of the test, the instructor advised me to relax, saying that the steering system in a modern car was very sensitive, and tension made steering more difficult. I was delighted when he told me I had passed.

Passing the IAM examination reduced my insurance premium by thirty percent, a substantial saving. I displayed the IAM badge on my car with satisfaction – and relief!

On reflection, I felt that passing the IAM examination had similarities to passing the MRCP examination required of trainee physicians in order to progress in their career, namely, doing the 'basics' very well, as opposed to the 'clever stuff'.

Certain other benefits came from the IAM training. On one occasion, I was stopped by the police when driving the three miles from the Royal Hospital to the Royal Infirmary. The driver's colleague asked, "Who, my good man, taught you to drive?" When I named the police officers who were the IAM instructors, they were a bit nonplussed but graciously told me to continue driving carefully!

Rotherham

1970s

Rotherham Hospital today

By 1972, I was ready to apply for a consultant's post and began considering my options. I wanted to return and work in India, but there were no suitable openings. Most people expected me to continue on the academic path, but I changed direction and opted to work in a district general hospital. Later, I realised the reason for this was a yearning for independence, to be able to do my own thing in my style, i.e. devote myself fully to clinical work, develop research and engage in teaching medical students and junior doctors. I had no interest in private practice.

My clinical experience in the UK was limited, having spent just over three years in research at Oxford. Consultants in those days were classed as general physicians who took care of patients with a wide variety of disorders. It was an invaluable experience and preparation for the coming years.

I was shortlisted for an interview at three centres in the UK but was turned down for lack of experience. And so it was that I applied to Rotherham for a consultant post that had been vacant for a couple of years. Many on the interview panel pointed to my lack of experience, but I was fortunate to have been selected in those days as a consultant at the relatively young age of thirty-two.

My wish was to specialise in gastroenterology, which was not a recognised speciality at the time. Later, many consultant physicians were allowed to indicate an area of interest and they could devote more time to this. Gastrointestinal endoscopy was rapidly increasing, so I was classed as a general physician with a special interest in gastroenterology, and over time was reclassified as a gastroenterologist.

Consultant interviews in those days were held at the Trent Regional Health Authority, the over-arching body that covered many hospitals. The interview panel consisted of several consultants from different centres in the UK and senior physicians from Rotherham. The 'neutral' chairman was Mr Jack Layden (later Sir Jack). Many pointed out that I lacked experience. When asked why I thought I could fulfil my duties, I replied that I had been unofficially 'working above my grade', and this, I enjoyed. When asked why I thought I could do the job, I replied, "I just feel lucky!" All panellists laughed, and I was appointed.

A few days later, I approached the Chief Medical Officer of Trent Regional Health Authority, asking for advice about what was expected of a consultant. His wise counsel was to go to the two hospitals I would be covering and to meet the people I would be working with. Then he asked me to live up to the faith that the other staff members had placed in me. I was surprised – and touched. This is the finest job description I have ever known. To rely on faith and morality is wonderful. Ever since I have strived, and realised that Rotherham is indeed my 'promised land' and that my instinctive choice was correct.

My first chief at the Royal Hospital in Sheffield told me that new consultants have a "honeymoon period", so when asking for equipment, expect that very little of your wish list will be given to you.

I could see in which direction endoscopy was developing. So, I asked for a gastroscope and a colonoscope. I had seen photos of a duodenoscope, necessary when the biliary tree has to be examined, but had never seen the instrument itself. I was lucky that everything that I had asked for was granted. I learnt that the chairman had insisted that my wish list be granted in full.

Instinctively I sensed opportunities, which later were to be fulfilled through the combination of wonderful supportive patients, senior consultants from whom I learnt much, and the members of the team I was building up. The hospital management was amazed that anyone would undertake research at a small place, so they encouraged me. As always, my wife Gouri gave me her full support.

10th January 1973 was my first working day at Rotherham. A small part of my time was spent at Montagu Hospital in Mexborough and the rest at Doncaster Gate Hospital, where Len Williams was the Head Porter. I was only thirty-two, young to hold a consultant post in those days, self-evidently inexperienced but full of hope and energy, striving to learn. Len sensed this and nurtured me in many ways with characteristic altruism. He was a very special, kind, gentle and ever-helpful man.

The Growth of Gastroscopy

I learnt this new technique working with my mentor at The Royal Infirmary in Sheffield. Peering down the gastroscope took me to a mesmerising new world! For the very first time, I could see duodenal ulcers, gastric ulcers and gastric cancers: one look and I could understand why our patients suffered. Furthermore, I could now take biopsies, particularly for gastric ulcers, and our pathologists could check for signs of cancer.

All gastroscopies then were done under sedation, and being a novice, it would take me up to twenty minutes to complete an examination. Another five to ten minutes were spent taking the patient off the couch onto a trolley or wheelchair to a recovery room nearby. With experience, I speeded it all up and brought the time down to five minutes, but this was difficult to sustain with the manpower we had.

Creating a laboratory

Len's office was at the far end of the main corridor. Whilst having a mug of tea with him, I mentioned that I would love to have a small laboratory to continue the earlier research work started at Sheffield. Len's office was adjacent to a large store room, formerly a laboratory. Len became aware that the contents would be removed from the room and advised me to approach our local manager to ask if we could use the vacated space.

Len and his porters commandeered old filing cabinets, chairs and cupboards, and the helpful people from the Estates Department fashioned a laboratory which I slowly fitted with second-hand equipment. Once again, fortune smiled on me: an experienced laboratory scientist, Mr M Ishaque, joined me, and several 'fun' years followed. It was the dawning of our research programmes.

During our conversations, I learnt that Len had left school at age fourteen to work on the railways. Later he became a miner, a 'ripper' on the coalface at Aldwarke Colliery, moving on to Cadeby. He could not continue after experiencing a bad injury, so he applied for a porter's position at Doncaster Gate Hospital. Such was his natural ability at 'man management' that he rose to be head porter, a position he was asked to continue at the new District General Hospital. With typical generosity, he chose the deputy post as he wanted a younger man to take the senior one. He was much loved by so many of the hospital staff that as a special gesture his retirement ceremony was held in the Board Room. Len retired in the autumn of 1982.

I remember the many times Len and I went on fishing trips with other members of the Endoscopy Unit to Bridlington, Filey and Flamborough. He would always be smartly dressed in a suit and tie, whereas the only certainty for me was my seasickness. On one occasion, lying at the bottom of the boat with the fish hook dangling overboard, I was the only one who caught a fish! All the others cried, "Unfair!" but once on land, Len would comfort me with his homemade sandwiches. The following week, jokes spread in the Endoscopy Unit: "What's brown and turns green?" This was a neat summary of my seasickness!

My dear friend Len passed away in 2004, aged 88.

Early research in Rotherham

Patients with very troublesome ulcers in the stomach or duodenum were traditionally treated in the hospital with bed rest, milk drips and soft foods, sometimes for several weeks. A major clinical trial with Carbenoxolone, derived from liquorice, showed that ulcers healed more quickly when treated with Carbenoxolone instead of a placebo.

Some patients developed oedema (the accumulation of fluid), and their blood potassium levels dropped, resembling the effects of aldosterone, a hormone released by the adrenal glands. So an alternative medication was developed, based on liquorice but devoid of the element causing side effects. It was named deglycyrrhizinised liquorice (DGL) and marketed as Ulcedal.

An interesting related story is that during the Napoleonic wars, Russian soldiers were forbidden to chew liquorice to relieve tummy pain for fear of dropsy (oedema) that might follow.

My early clinical research at Rotherham was done with my endoscopy mentor, Dr C Derek Holdsworth, from whom I learnt much. We set out to assess the therapeutic value of DGL. There were some reports that the drug was effective, but the studies were small; this can produce misleading results. Our study was much larger: ninety-six patients were recruited and randomly allocated to treatment with the drug or an identical placebo. After four weeks, there were no differences in outcome in the proportions with complete healing (assessed by either gastroscopy or radiology), reduction in ulcer area, or clinical improvement.

As the senior investigator, I expected Dr Holdsworth to present the results. With extraordinary generosity, however, he persuaded me to present these results at the British Society of Gastroenterology meeting in Canterbury in 1976. I rehearsed thoroughly with Dr Holdsworth and made my presentation, which seemed to be well received. Ultimately, I could not help quipping, "I only hope the DGL team does not lynch me!"

Today, clinical research studies are regulated by law so that misleading or inaccurate claims cannot be advanced. Many complain about the bureaucracy involved, yet its benefits are worth the trouble. The subject is now vast, so I have restricted myself to the studies my team and I have been involved with.

Acid suppression and ulcer healing: the journey from Metiamide to Cimetidine

Hormones mediate their effect through specific receptors, as do medications. In those days, two types of histamine receptors were characterised, H1 and H2. The former mediates allergy reactions, whereas H2 influences acid secretion. This led to the big drive to develop H2 receptor antagonists, which could be used in treating duodenal ulcers by speeding up the relief of symptoms and healing.

Metiamide was the first oral H2 receptor antagonist (H2RA) found to be effective with duodenal ulcers. Shortly before its launch, however, the manufacturers, Smith, Kline and French (SK&F), noted that a small number of patients had developed neutropenia, a reduction in a particular type of white blood cell essential to counteract infections.

This proved to be the end of Metiamide since those prescribed the drug might succumb to infection. There was an alternative that hastened the drug's end, namely, major surgery, the age-old standard treatment until that point.

It is extraordinary how fate, luck and chance have played their parts in my life. Dr Holdsworth told me about these developments when Metiamide was being evaluated, and I repeatedly wrote to SK&F but never received a reply. Quite by chance, SK&F had a backup drug, Cimetidine. Crucially, the head of the clinical research team attended the meeting where I presented the results on deglycyrrhizinised liquorice (DGL). In light of this, he sent his clinical research team members, both clinicians and scientists, to meet me and check if I was in a position to participate in a double-blind study of cimetidine against a placebo in patients with duodenal ulcers.

From this point onwards, our clinical trial programme increased rapidly. Senior clinicians were understandably hesitant to participate, as they were familiar with the Metiamide saga. However, being young and inexperienced, I was very eager to get involved! The SK&F team visited me at Doncaster Gate Hospital. It was pleasing to see the endoscopy set-up, which allowed a steadily increasing number of gastroscopies to be done in a half-day, leading to open access gastroscopy.

It was during the halcyon days of Cimetidine that I came to meet the SK&F sales representative covering our area. He let the evidence of a drug's efficacy speak for itself, balancing it against potential side effects. More importantly, he nurtured the young within his own company and consultants appointed prematurely like myself! He played a major part in the development of gastroenterology at Rotherham.

In those early days, the general practitioner would usually refer a patient with ulcer-like symptoms to a consultant for an outpatient appointment. Our practice was rapidly changing, however, and we soon introduced open-access gastroscopy. Gastroscopy as a first step allowed us to see the patient soon after referral and, whilst still symptomatic, the 'golden' period, as it were when we were most likely to make a diagnosis – or to rule out ulcer as a cause of the patient's symptoms.

A multicentre study was designed involving several centres. Rotherham had recruited the majority of patients, but custom dictates that senior people present the results of any study as they carry authority. Nevertheless, I was generously allowed to present our results at the second conference on H2RA held in 1976 at The Royal College of Physicians in London.

The second conference on H2RA: Royal College of Physicians - 1976

The response to Cimetidine proved to be a vast improvement; sixty-one per cent of patients experienced complete healing within four weeks. More importantly, from the patients' point of view, swift relief was reported from the troublesome pain which had often wrecked their lives. In keeping with the majority view, I assumed naively that their disease was cured. In many centres, patients were discharged, but 'something' within me urged otherwise; as a consequence, in my usual 'independent' way, I continued checking my patients' insides every few months, which, unsurprisingly, got me into hot water with the authorities!

There were two crucial findings: first, extending treatment beyond four weeks would heal many ulcers still active. Second, when treatment stopped, ulcers would recur in most patients. Acid secretion is triggered by food that buffers or neutralises the acid. For those whose work allows them to sleep through the night, only a small amount of acid is needed, just sufficient to keep the stomach sterile. As a result, Cimetidine at bedtime, even at a low dose, successfully controlled the disease in most patients.

Cimetidine proved to be a great success, both clinically and commercially, as, at last, a really effective medical treatment was available, reducing the need for surgery. Its commercial name, Tagamet, was decided upon using the words 'an**tag**onist' and 'ci**met**idine'!

I would like to mention some of my intriguing cases with suspected ulcer problems from whom I learnt a great deal.

Acid Rain

I recall this story which happened in the Surgical Unit in Vellore. The patient had undergone a partial gastrectomy for a duodenal ulcer, as was then common. To everyone's surprise and dismay, however, he then developed fistulae at various sites and ultimately passed away. At autopsy, the pancreas showed islet cell hyperplasia. Question: Was this an example of a true Zollinger-Ellison Syndrome (ZES) or a variant? The entity of ZES had recently been described in The Lancet by R M Zollinger and E H Ellison.

I came across patients who were afflicted by greatly increased acid secretion which could not be fully controlled by Cimetidine, the first major anti-secretory drug. The result was that the ulcers continued, often penetrating the wall of the gut, leaking ultimately into other gut loops and to the exterior. A high proportion died as a result. At autopsy, the pancreas would be swollen. Another feature was the occurrence of ulcers in the jejunum, the portion of the gut beyond the duodenum.

At my clinic at Montagu Hospital, I had seen a patient with troublesome tummy pain who had a large number of white duodenal erosions extending fairly far down. Other than my description of these findings in the notes there was no striking feature.

Sometime later a GP requested that I see Mr DS on a domiciliary visit. He had recently returned from a holiday in Malta, where he had developed "tummy problems" which continued. Gastroscopy showed a large number of ulcers and erosions. Although there were some ulcers in the stomach, the majority were in the duodenum and extended even further down into the jejunum. I sensed his problems would not be easy to treat so I admitted him to the Princess Mary Ward at Doncaster Gate Hospital.

I was intrigued by ZES and began to study it. It is characterised by an excess of gastrin, a hormone which stimulates the stomach to secrete acid even when this is not needed. I also learnt that gastrin can be measured in venous blood. The assay was carried out at the Hammersmith Hospital. DS's gastrin level, measured in blood taken from the arm, was high. It seemed likely the source was a tumour, probably in the pancreas as had been described in the literature.

The nearest CT scanner was in Manchester. I knew the consultant in charge as we had been colleagues at the Royal Hospital in Sheffield. Along with DS, the Consultant Radiologist at Rotherham, and a medical student, I drove to Manchester. To my surprise, the scan did not show a tumour or indeed any other abnormality.

DS's ulcers recurred, even whilst continuing Cimetidine at high doses, and gastrin levels rose. My surgical colleague operated on him and noted a tumour at the pancreatic tail. This gave the chance of taking blood samples for gastrin from surrounding vessels, such as the splenic and hepatic veins, and vessels in the pancreas.

There was an amazing interventional radiologist at Leeds who was able to carry out trans-hepatic blood sampling within the abdomen. In effect, a catheter is guided up the inferior vena cava (the large vein carrying blood from the lower body to the heart) and from there guided into smaller vessels. His intervention showed that whilst the blood from peripheral veins had normal levels of gastrin, those at the centre might have much higher levels. He showed this in DS's case, which opened up my thinking.

DS put up a magnificent resistance but sadly died. His family was very grateful for the help we had given and asked me to attend his funeral. I was deeply moved and commented that DS's fortitude and courage were inspirational, a hero from whom I learnt much.

As has happened in my life on several occasions, one patient's story reminds me of other patients with similar problems. ZES is uncommon yet within a decade we had come across several patients with this condition, as well as variants.

Reflecting on DS reminded me of other patients who had similar problems.

TH: Montagu patient. His endoscopic appearances were similar to those of DS. So, I investigated him retrospectively.

An eighteen or nineteen-year-old unusually thin girl with refractory duodenal ulcer whom I had treated with Cimetidine. I *think* there was a suspicion of a ZES variant, named 'antral G-cell hyperplasia'. She finally underwent partial gastrectomy.

PP (in his early thirties) had presented with a jejunal perforation; the clinical presentation of itself virtually confirmed ZES. The patient was considerably overweight, and we wondered if his ghrelin levels were raised (ghrelin is a hormone which we planned to send to Hammersmith Hospital for assay). He later died of cardiomyopathy.

SB was the last one I can remember. I referred him to a young consultant at Derby as they had access to endoscopic ultrasound (EUS), which we lacked at that time in Sheffield. He removed some of the gastrinomas from the duodenum. Whilst our unit's work continued and expanded, I have not seen another patient with ZES, typical or otherwise.

Perforated duodenal ulcer: Illusion or aura?

A group of doctors just a few years younger than me elected to work in my unit, attracted by its 'style' of training within which every person's view mattered and was actively sought.

My houseman, a very fit squash player, was suddenly struck down with severe abdominal pain whilst on the ward. The surgical registrar rushed to see him; he made a preliminary diagnosis of a perforated duodenal ulcer and wanted to operate immediately. I was not convinced that there was actually a perforation and so suggested a gastroscopy as a first step. The registrar was hesitant but finally agreed.

The gastroscopy showed the inner surface of the stomach was pale, almost white. Suddenly, a small jet of bile appeared in the stomach, having been refluxed back from the duodenum. The only times I had seen such an appearance was in patients who had already undergone major stomach surgery. This did not apply to him. I suddenly recalled hearing about a similar appearance in abdominal migraine[10] but had never come across it myself.

We had a long chat back on the ward and he recalled having recurrent tummy pain and vomiting as a child but not as an adult, so understandably had forgotten about the problem. I came to know later that his sister had suffered troublesome bouts of tummy pain when young, but that the attacks still troubled her as an adult.

It was a relief to all of us, as he was spared a major operation to find a perforation which had not occurred!

This was a wonderful learning experience for me: when the clinical picture is not clear and life is not under immediate threat, it is wise to 'wait and see'. By way of contrast, in those days if a

---

[10] www.bmj.com/content/360/bmj.k179

patient experienced a massive life-threatening bleed from their stomach, an urgent operation was necessary to stop it.

The Question of Transfusion

The Perspiring Priest

The patient, a middle-aged priest, was ill, pale and wet with perspiration. He felt dizzy and had passed dark, tarry stools a few times. Bravely, he tried to maintain composure but his mounting fear was impossible to hide.

These events took place one afternoon in the mid-1970s on the Princess Mary Ward at the old Doncaster Gate Hospital in the centre of Rotherham.

I drew up a chair beside him to discuss the nature of his problem and the need for a gastroscopy. I told him that he had lost a lot of blood internally and I needed to find out where he had bled from to decide what needed to be done. He had difficulty believing this for there was no red blood to be seen anywhere.

Then followed a discussion on melaena, which understandably perplexed him. It is easy to understand when one vomits bright red blood. More often, the blood, rich in protein, passes down the gut and in effect gets digested, its colour changing from red to black. The commonest reason for such bleeding is a peptic ulcer, either in the stomach or much more often in the duodenum, which lies just beyond the stomach.

I explained what a gastroscopy involved, which troubled him even further. I told him that I had learnt the technique of gastroscopy from my mentor based at The Royal Infirmary in Sheffield. His encouragement along with that of my senior colleagues in Rotherham had helped me to develop the service.

The priest reluctantly agreed to have the examination yet he still had reservations and asked me whether I had done many such examinations before. I told him I had done several but mainly in patients who came to see me for tummy pain suggesting an ulcer. He was alarmed that he was the first patient to be examined for suspected bleeding.

He was taken to the operation theatre and, after sedating him, I carried out a gastroscopy, which confirmed that he had a duodenal ulcer.

I saw him back in the ward a couple of hours later. He thanked me somewhat groggily as the effects of sedation were still present. I thanked him for having arranged Divine guidance!

My surgical colleagues saw him and felt that as the bleeding had stopped, there was no need for immediate operation. He completed the blood transfusion, stayed on the ward for a few more days and went home feeling much better.

Bleeding in a Jehovah's Witness at Doncaster Gate Hospital

The forty-year-old patient was surrounded by his family; a lady whom I think was a nurse along with a slim gentleman with a limp urging the patient to be steadfast in his beliefs. I phoned the Deputy Hospital Manager for guidance. He rushed up and wrote extensive notes of the sequence of events, and a colleague countersigned as a witness.

I pleaded with the patient's son, asking if he was aware of the consequences. He looked at me scornfully, commenting that he was fully aware. I tried to talk to him alone but he refused.

The family wanted everything done, even surgery, but *not* to have a blood transfusion at any time.

It was dreadful to see the patient becoming progressively paler, sweating and breathless, as the sympathetic nervous system was in overdrive. Breathing oxygen did not help. I considered giving him a sedative intravenously, as in his poor state it would not have been absorbed if given by mouth.

I stayed with him for some hours before returning home. He passed away shortly thereafter.

Sometime later another patient, also a Jehovah's Witness, was admitted. Again the 'nurse' and the man with a limp were with him. At gastroscopy, I saw a duodenal ulcer, still oozing. I discussed the matter with my surgical colleague. He took the patient to the theatre and over-sewed the ulcer. As it happened, blood transfusion was not necessary but it has to be stated that in those days no surgeon would have dared to operate without having cross-matched blood at hand. Thankfully the patient recovered.

This was in my younger days, and the loss of the first patient upset me deeply. The second patient troubled me: what if he needed a blood transfusion? In more recent times, however, methods to stop bleeding from an ulcer have advanced greatly, for example by using clips passed down through a gastroscope, which could then be placed on the bleeding vessel, thus blocking it.

An earlier event from my college days

I recall a patient from my rural posting days in Vellore. One evening a very ill young woman was brought to the little hospital in a bullock cart. She was in a great deal of abdominal pain and was rapidly going downhill.

As this was an abdominal emergency, it was the chief who did the operation. He made a wide incision and we realised that the lady had a ruptured ectopic pregnancy and was bleeding profusely.

The nearest blood bank was at our main hospital about forty-five miles away. It was a perilous situation. I remembered reading about bleeding from an ectopic pregnancy and the blood collecting in the pouch of Douglas:[11] if blood was not available for transfusion then, in an emergency, this blood could be used.

We rapidly tried to syphon the blood into a sterile blood bottle and transfused her with this. It seemed a miracle to us that it worked, and we managed to save the poor lady who was able to leave the hospital and go home in a few days. I realise that this was an early form of auto-transfusion.

I have always put the patient's interest above all else, and in my young days, their survival was my principal aim. It was only much later in life, as maturity gradually developed, I came to realise survival alone might not be the best course. Admittedly this was not in the context of gastrointestinal bleeding in the young, but often in those nearing the end of life. I have given examples of this in other chapters concerning cardiopulmonary resuscitation (CPR) in those whose prognosis was very poor. Palliative care was still many years in the future.

I agonised over the moral issues raised by these patients. Specifically, the rights of the individual patient to do as he/she chooses; is it deliberate assault for the doctor to do otherwise, or should it be considered a heroic action done in difficult circumstances? It is one thing when a very old patient refuses treatment and asks only to be made comfortable. For younger patients, however, I would strive to help, even if against the expressed wishes of the patient, on the grounds they are not well-placed to make rational judgements. Some would call me arrogant, understandably, but I would find it almost impossible not to try and help those whom I could.

---

[11] The pouch of Douglas is an anatomical structure named after the Scottish anatomist James Douglas. It is a bag-shaped extension of the peritoneum (a membrane that lines the insides of the abdomen and pelvis) located between the posterior wall of the uterus and the rectum.

Hypnosis in Gastroenterology

Gastroenterologists were becoming increasingly aware of the 'brain-gut axis' which, as the name implies, indicates the degree to which the two organs influence each other. I recalled the aphorism learnt at medical school, "The abdomen is the mirror of the mind".

I came to learn that a consultant gastroenterologist had achieved results by using hypnotherapy. I found this intriguing and wanted to learn more. I met with him, a delightful gentleman, and learnt a lot about managing illnesses without drugs or operations. He demonstrated his hypnosis technique to a large audience at one of our postgraduate meetings. Several of his patients, all ladies, kindly volunteered to attend. I was struck by how rapidly he was able to hypnotise each of them.

Learning hypnosis, a new frontier for me

By good fortune, a hypnotherapy course had been arranged at Rotherham Hospital; this involved a primer over a weekend and a refresher one month later. The three principal speakers were fully trained surgeons who had later moved to general practice. The attendees, many GPs, were puzzled by my presence, and some who knew me well wondered why I was attending as they thought I would have considered hypnotherapy to be mumbo-jumbo! They had a point, but I assured them that I was always willing to learn!

It was a very interesting day, where we learnt to hypnotise each other. I decided to try hypnosis on the following Monday's gastroscopy list. The first patient presented with ulcer-like symptoms but also had chronic lung disease; this rendered him breathless, making gastroscopy under sedation risky. So I tried to apply my new learning, but the nurses and porters looked mystified! Within a few minutes, the gentleman was hypnotised and for the first time in my life, I was able to carry out the procedure without any sedation!

The following week another patient also had troublesome respiratory problems and yet after several minutes of attempted hypnosis nothing happened. It turned out he was not wearing his hearing aid!

I used hypnosis on several occasions after that, and this included a patient who demanded sedation yet was terrified of needles.

Reflections

Hypnosis and hypnotherapy may well have been regarded as 'mysticism' (the polite language for 'mumbo-jumbo') in the past but this is less the case today. A corresponding example perhaps is acupuncture, dismissed as nonsense when I was a young consultant, but now used widely by physiotherapists and some anaesthetists.

On reflection, I realise we now have a better understanding of the links between the mind, conscious and subconscious, and derangements in human physiology. Intuitively one can understand how a drug works but less so in the case of hypnosis. Is the response the effect of the hypnotherapist or the susceptibility of the patient? The medical consultation is unusual in the sense that both the 'seeker' and 'giver' of help are fellow human beings; one in possession of technical information, the other may well possess a deeper insight and a richer life experience without the technical knowledge. Over time, I have learnt that when empathy, respect and trust for each other develop, the consultation is more rewarding for both. This can be sensed mutually but is more difficult to 'measure'.

Moreover, we have undertaken scientific studies which showed psychotherapy has benefits in patients with troublesome abdominal symptoms labelled as irritable bowel syndrome.

In the context of hypnosis, two quotations appeal to me:

"*The heart has its reasons that reason knows nothing of*"

Blaise Pascal, 17th Century French scientist, mathematician and priest.

"*We live on an island surrounded by a sea of ignorance. As our island of knowledge grows, so does the shore of our ignorance.*"

John Archibald Wheeler (1911-2008), an American theoretical physicist with a particular interest in relativity.

Domiciliary Visits

In the early years, domiciliary visits (DVs) were an important feature of my life. The fact that I can still recall some of those visits indicates the impact these had.

The rationale for DVs was that both the referring general practitioner (GP) and the consultant could see the patient at home, a setting very different from a hospital outpatient clinic or the wards.

We were expected to do four or five DV consultations 'free of charge', other than for reimbursement of mileage costs; thereafter we would receive payment for consultations. Both GP and consultant would keep a register, and after submitting the necessary documentation the consultant would receive payment.

In those days the only way of locating directions to a patient's home was by using the Automobile Association's (AA) road atlas; satellite navigation was in the distant future.

I was asked to visit a patient who had become ill with an unusual combination of sudden deafness together with a lump in his tummy. I discussed the problem with Gouri, who at the time was a trainee haematologist; she advised me to bear in mind hyperviscosity. Blood contains many different types of cells and proteins, the latter mainly albumin. Immunoglobulins, large key defence molecules, are also present; when in excess, the blood thickens, i.e. it becomes more viscous, slowing blood flow.

The patient was lying on the floor, his distressed wife trying to comfort him. The fact that he was on the floor was an advantage as it made it simpler to examine his tummy; if he had been on a bed, he would have sunk into the mattress when I was pressing on the tummy, making it more difficult to detect subtle changes.

The liver is in the upper right quadrant of the abdomen; when enlarged it extends down and its edge can be seen when the patient takes a deep breath. Further information can be gained by examining the surface, for example detecting nodules, which would point towards cirrhosis or tumour deposits.

The spleen is located on the left, tucked away at the back. It is much smaller than the liver and has a characteristic notch at its upper edge. When enlarged, its tip extends downwards and the notch can be more readily felt.

Whilst a medical student at the Christian Medical College and later as a doctor, I had the opportunity to feel the enlarged spleen in many patients caused by a variety of problems; Kala-Azar for instance, caused mainly by parasites, or by chronic myeloid leukaemia.

The gentleman I had been asked to see had a truly massive spleen, and a possible cause was leukaemia of the myeloid type – characterised by an excess of neutrophils, a type of white blood cell necessary to defend against infection.

I arranged for an urgent transfer to a consultant haematologist. Regrettably, I never got to know of the final outcome.

As previously mentioned, DVs were usually initiated by GPs. In one particular instance, things were 'back to front'!

I happened to be at Doncaster Gate Hospital and was summoned by a consultant in the Accident and Emergency Department to see a middle-aged gentleman who noticed his fingers rapidly darkening, as though he had 'chilblains'. This condition occurs when it is cold but the weather was pleasant: the combination raised the possibility of cryoglobulinaemia, a rarity, 'small text' stuff which sticks in my mind! It is characterised by circulating globulins starting to sludge and then crystallise, thereby slowing down the arterial circulation and eventually blocking it, and this in some people can lead to gangrene.

The patient's GP was my friend Barrie Hillman so I phoned him urgently. He referred the patient to the haematology department for specialist management. That was the only instance I have knowingly encountered cryoglobulinaemia.

I carried out a DV on a very fit-looking man who inexplicably would suddenly become short of breath. It was a pleasant afternoon so to observe the event we decided to go for a walk, accompanied by his son and their dog. Unfortunately, his GP was very busy at his clinic so could not join us. We walked at a steady pace and then agreed to try a gentle jog. It started well but within thirty to forty yards he suddenly stopped, sank to the ground, leaned back on his hands and started to take deep, gasping breaths. He recovered after about twenty to thirty minutes. Regrettably, I did not record precise times; I could have kicked myself, for this was a wonderful opportunity which would have been difficult to reproduce at the hospital. Further testimony indeed for the value of a domiciliary visit.

A senior instructor and manager at the gym told me that I had seen his mother on a DV. She had graciously offered me a cup of tea but I had had to decline as I was short of time. When I got home I wrote to thank her for her kindness and generosity and apologised for not being able to take it up; I also assured her I would visit again. I was amazed that she had saved the letter, which her son showed me on my next visit to the gym. The very letter I had sent. I was deeply moved.

A row of bungalows had been built in Denaby Main, the next village from Mexborough. I was asked to see an elderly man but I had to be guided to his bungalow by others as the house numbers were not marked. For that reason, he had not left his home for over a week fearing he would be unable to retrace his steps!

I was asked to visit an ex-miner, who was upstairs in bed when I arrived. A polite man, he wanted to greet me at the door and came down on his bottom, step by step. This was extraordinary, both brave and determined.

On another occasion, I was asked to see a man at Wath upon Dearne as his health was rapidly declining. The house was in a mess, with cigarette butts, dirty plates and various other items strewn all around. There was a half-eaten sandwich, which I got the impression he had shared with his docile dog.

I examined his tummy and it was clear 'something' was wrong as it felt full, stiff and tender. I admitted him for gastroscopy and at the examination saw a remarkable sight which I had never seen before. His stomach was studded with what I can only describe as 'micro-volcanoes', small hillocks with their tops capped with mucopurulent material. Biopsies confirmed these were tumour deposits which had spread from cancer in the lung. This was before we had palliative care. He passed away shortly, peacefully in his sleep.

I did domiciliary visits as soon as possible, bearing in mind that when away from the hospital I would have less time to see patients already admitted under my care. If the weather was good, I would try and do the visit on a weekend, taking my wife and our son in the back seat of my car. Many patients were aware that we had recently had our first child, Sonny. One lady came out to the car, tickled his chubby cheeks and gave him a five-pound note, which she could ill afford; such was her generosity. I politely returned it and thanked her for her kindness. The next-door neighbour came across and brought some vegetables from his garden, a phenomenon which occurred at several other such DVs.

I learnt that DVs were both a medical and a social interaction. In all medical interactions I have regarded myself as a servant of the patient, who was frequently older, often much older, and had far more 'life experience', and indeed plain 'common sense': from them I learnt a great deal.

The Story of 'The Hut'

As my clinical work increased, so did my wish for a small laboratory for experimental investigations.

The hut's story is a long one, spanning the period from 1975 until its demise in 2018/19. The laboratory had started at Doncaster Gate Hospital and its functions transferred to the new hospital in early 1979. The kindly and most helpful deputy manager gave us a small freestanding building at the back of the hospital, previously used by the Estates Department to store garden equipment. This became part of the Gastroenterology Department, affectionately nicknamed 'the hut'!

The Hut

It passed through many phases in its development but remained at all times an exciting place, as our work continually explored new frontiers where risks were high with no assurance of success. This turbulent territory was our research 'home', basically the 'nerve centre' for all our work.

Medicine is based on science, which advances through research; its practice, however, is an art. Research is necessarily carried out in academic centres; this often requires major funding, up to half a million pounds or more perhaps depending on the equipment and personnel required.

The Sheffield-based Trent Regional Health Authority (TRHA) was well aware of the value of research. They also knew that consultant physicians like me were 'generalists' who looked after patients with a wide range of disorders. Nevertheless, several of us had special areas of interest, gastroenterology in my case. Knowing that they would have little time for research, they kept the 'spirit of enquiry' alive by providing small grants of £2500-£5000 to cover laboratory expenses. The catch was that the consultant/investigator had to find funds to cover the salary of anyone recruited to support the work.

During my clinical years whilst a medical student, I was fascinated by the wide range of problems that patients suffered with. Through the influence of a charismatic teacher, I developed a particular interest in duodenal ulcer (DU) disease and its relationship to acid secretion. The established facts at the time were that DU occurs only where there is acid and that maximal acid secretion was higher in DU than in healthy people. Initially, the cause for the difference was unclear, but we subsequently learnt that people with DU had many more parietal cells (the source of acid) compared with normal subjects. It was only later that the work of several people, including ourselves, was to show that other factors made an important contribution to the development of DU, for example, the impact of *Helicobacter pylori* (Hp), amongst others.

The Arrival of Mr Mohammed Ishaque

Mr Ishaque

I was fortunate to receive a £2500 grant from TRHA, and this had far-reaching consequences. The grant brought together Mr Ishaque (MI), a laboratory scientist, and me; for both of us, Rotherham proved to be our 'promised land'! MI joined me at the old hospital and we were able to continue together in the new one. He had sent numerous applications to many centres in the UK, and Rotherham was the first one to invite him for a chat.

District general hospitals (DGH) were created to provide a wide range of clinical services for the population they covered. Finances would often be strained, with departments competing against each other. Unsurprisingly, many thought research was an unnecessary 'luxury', all the more so when the nature of the work was laboratory-based.

The hospital had to fund MI's salary, a delicate issue as there were many other competing demands. Nevertheless, our far-seeing Treasurer saw the potential value of the work and supported us. The TRHA gave us a further grant, and this extended MI's tenure. Having retained MI on consecutive grants, there was a moral obligation (as opposed to a legal requirement) to make his post permanent, allowing us to plan for the long-term. Small-scale funding came through collaborative research with the pharmaceutical industry and donations.

Hardworking and loyal, MI was engaging and made friends with many people who, in their turn, helped us in several ways.

Our scientific equipment was mostly second-hand, lovingly reconditioned by our Estates Department's engineers, who were all caught up in the novelty of our enterprise. This, in turn, steadily expanded the range of our work.

On one occasion, we were informed that a number of infusion pumps from the dialysis centre at the Northern General Hospital had been discarded as they had been superseded by smaller machines. We arranged to collect the pumps, and to my surprise, they were 'state of the art' machines which we could use to measure the effect of a new anti-secretory drug, then called LS 519 (and later, Pirenzepine).

Equipping our laboratory with furniture was a problem as at that time we had little money. Fate in the form of the lovely deputy supplies officer came to our aid. There was a lot of furniture and similar items that the Lodge Moor Hospital in Sheffield was discarding. On 'D-Day' there would be a "strange gap" in continuity; specifically, no organisation or person would be responsible for the equipment, much of which would be thrown away. We were told that the Rotherham Hospital van "just might happen to call at Lodge Moor Hospital", and if we happened to be there at the same time we might be able to help ourselves to the items we wanted! Accordingly, MI and I went in my car, met the driver, and indicated the items we wanted. He and his supporting crew put these in the van and delivered them to the hut the next day! In addition, I came to learn that the old centrifuge that I had often used as a lecturer at the Royal Hospital Professorial Unit was to be discarded. Arrangements were made for it to be delivered to the hut, where it was put to use almost non-stop.

In my early days, I got the impression there had been little progress in treating duodenal ulcer other than with antacids, which was entirely logical. Acid secretion, we learned later, is controlled by the histamine H2 pathway; at that time, however, there was no means of accessing it to reduce secretion. Acid secretion is also influenced, to a lesser degree, by the cholinergic pathway, for which anticholinergic drugs had become available.

I found an old Martindale Pharmacopeia and studied the antacids section, noting the names of magnesium trisilicate and aluminium hydroxide. Each had the potential to cause side effects: diarrhoea with magnesium and constipation with aluminium. I wondered whether or not, in a fifty-fifty mixture, the side effects would cancel each other out! In a pilot programme, the head of our hospital pharmacy produced the specific combination, which became known as the 'KDB Mixture'!

Making KDB Mixture cost far less than the antacids commercially produced. It crossed my mind that we could use income generated by selling antacids to support the pharmacy and our expanding research. This was at the time of Mrs Margaret Thatcher's Government (1979-90), which ruled that state-supported activity such as the NHS would not be allowed to compete with private enterprise initiatives, a point of view I could understand. As it happened, the Government produced a 'black list' of drugs on the grounds that several companies were selling antacids, some at high prices, which did not translate into greater clinical benefit. As a result, commercially manufactured antacids were 'dumped' into hospitals.

I mentioned earlier that the commercial products were superior in some respects, possessing, for example, a better taste and texture and maintaining a capacity to mix well when shaken. In contrast,

KDB Mixture tended to settle at the bottom of the bottle, but it was cheaper.

On reflection in later years, I wondered from time to time if our attempt at manufacturing antacids had been futile. I certainly accept that we could not match antacids commercially produced, even if at a fraction of the price. Nevertheless, it was a wonderful learning experience and showed that when our team put its mind to a project, many good things happened.

The commercially available preparations combined various types of antacid constituents. One which stood out, using the same constituents as KDB Mixture and in similar proportions, was hydroxytalcite, marketed by Roussel Laboratories as Altacite. Their Medical Director agreed to a pilot comparative study and generously gave us some funds.

We assessed hydroxytalcite's neutralising properties under laboratory conditions. The results were ranked by the ability to neutralise fully, along with its speed of action. On these criteria, magnesium trisilicate ranked first, Altacite second and aluminium hydroxide third.

We submitted our report, complete with hand-drawn graphs (this was in the days before computer graphics), to the TRHA as this was our first venture. The reviewer criticised us on the grounds that it added nothing to the literature. Research is competitive; publication, therefore, demands up-to-date information; no quarter is given to those who fail to provide it! Nevertheless, as has often happened in my life, such setbacks led to major developments, from time to time, in unexpected directions.

We appointed our own librarian; her salary would be cross-charged to my research funds. Soon the hut became a repository of books, a wide range of scientific journals, and specialist publications from the pharmaceutical industry, which went to great depth to support their products. Still back in pre-computer days, she devoted enormous time and effort to index these items manually, sharing our view that we should never be caught short of current knowledge!

Our specialist gastroenterology literature collection expanded and became a source for the region. Indeed, people from academic institutions began using our facilities.

Pepsin: A turning point

In addition to acid, the stomach secretes pepsin, a digestive enzyme that breaks down dairy products, eggs and, importantly, meat. This made us wonder at an intuitive level if acid and pepsin working together might play a major role in developing duodenal ulcers. As a result, we directed our efforts to its accurate measurement; only at this point did we start to investigate differences in DU patients compared to healthy subjects. We used the radial diffusion assay (RDA) and compared its performance with the existing gold standard. At the end of a lot of effort and time, the RDA proved not to be as good as the gold standard. We considered it a learning experience which gave us greater confidence to pursue further experimental studies. The generosity of many people in different parts of the UK and the USA was extraordinary and humbling.

Measuring pepsin: A helping hand

The clarified zone surrounding the well can be measured in the RDA, but precision is not easy when using a ruler. We, therefore, needed a photo enlarger, which our Estates Department managed to persuade the supplier to make available at half price (about twelve pounds). Looking at these sums today, this might seem trivial, but in our early days, we had minimal funds. This represents yet another example of how so many people supported us.

To maximise accuracy, we would turn off all lights. We now had large pictures of the well, and the surrounding clear zone could be measured with a ruler. This was the first publication produced by MI and myself.[12] It may not seem much, but it was an important encouraging first step, and we felt that more would follow.

MI was devoted to his work, and together we often worked late into the night. His wife phoned me one day to say the poor chap was unwell. I presumed he was down with 'flu' so I requested him to rest well and let me know when he wanted to return. However, he did not improve. Concerned, a very dear mutual friend and I called his home, and we were horrified to see how ill he was, racked with pain all over his body. We admitted him immediately and found that he had developed septicaemia, the infection spreading to his bones at various sites, causing abscesses (osteomyelitis). He was started on antibiotics, which had to be continued for a long period. The abscesses were drained by an orthopaedic surgeon, another mutual friend. There were also several unexplained neurological features which raised concern that there may be co-existing cancer, its primary site yet to be determined. The neurophysiologist conducted urgent studies, favouring infection rather than a tumour, a huge relief. MI coped bravely with his problems, enjoyed hydrotherapy and gradually began to recover. We were both able to look forward to resuming our working together.

Awkwardly at about this time, I suffered a heart attack and had to be admitted to the Northern General Hospital for urgent surgery. Within hours of my admission, MI came to visit me, struggling to get up the stairs. I was overcome by emotion and hugged him.

We both recovered and resumed our work, which steadily expanded.

One afternoon MI came to my office to discuss some aspects of our work before returning to the laboratory. I had arranged to collect

---

[12] An assessment of the radial diffusion method for the measurement of pepsin in gastric secretion and its comparison with the haemoglobin substrate colorimetric method. M Ishaque, KD Bardhan. *Clin Chim Acta* 1978;87:259-63

some papers from him before going to Sheffield for a meeting. As I drove to the laboratory, I noticed someone had collapsed nearby. Rushing out, I was horrified to see it was my friend. The 'crash call' was made, and I began external cardiac massage, which we continued in the Casualty, but to no avail. He died on 22 April 1986, aged 52.

The sudden death of MI touched many as he had a huge circle of friends, both at Rotherham and further afield. Several people approached me to offer their condolences. There was a groundswell of opinion that his passing should be marked by a memorial lecture, which I gave one evening in the lecture theatre of our hospital. The place was packed, and several wrote to me afterwards asking for additional information on some of the work we did.

This was a time of high productivity; the output of results contributed to our growing understanding of the nature of peptic ulcer disease. A consultant gastroenterologist at Derby commented at the end of my invited talk, "Based on square footage, this hut must be one of the most productive centres in the UK." Our hut was a place of great productivity, which was possible before the age of complete management control.

A similar observation was made by a distinguished gastroenterologist in London when he invited me to speak on 'Research in a District General Hospital'. After the loss of Mr Ishaque, we continued with our work and expanded in different directions. It was not always easy, less because of technical problems but more as I was repeatedly "told off" for straining the resources, i.e. doing too many endoscopies. High-volume endoscopy brought the hospital a lot of funds and served as a 'cash cow' to support other departments, but this was almost never acknowledged. Little wonder my host commented on the fact that the presentation had a lot of "raw emotion". It certainly did!

I have now been retired for some years. Looking back, I have sometimes wondered, "Would I do this again?" My answer is 'yes', but I would try to spend more time with my wife and our family.

Occasionally we bought new equipment, the first item being a Beckman pH meter to measure the neutralising power of different antacids (pH is the technical term to indicate acidity or alkalinity). The glass pH electrode was large, the size of a thick fountain pen, as was conventional at the time. Some weeks later, the Beckman salesman visited again and showed what seemed to be a nasogastric tube with a glass attachment at the end; this turned out to be a miniaturised pH probe. I asked him why it was made. He replied that one of their 'boffins' had made the device "out of curiosity". He then asked if I would like to keep it and think of ways I might want to use it. A few days later, it dawned on me that this was a novel piece of engineering as the tube and glass bead were narrow enough to pass down the throat and into the stomach. With great excitement, our first PhD student used it on himself, measuring his own stomach acidity for several minutes; the first time I have ever seen it being done. The device gave us a novel way of measuring acidity instantaneously.

We could now study the effect of food, antacids and so forth. This soon led to measuring acidity day and night, usually for about twenty-six hours, a major breakthrough; for now, we could assess the 'circadian rhythm' of stomach acidity. All cells of the body are regulated by a 'biological time clock'. Acid secretion in the healthy is greatly reduced at night, leaving behind only a small amount to keep the stomach sterile. In contrast, patients with DU continue to secrete acid both day and night.

The work expanded on circadian pH rhythms, and our student gained a PhD. This was to transform our thinking about duodenal ulcer disease.

Throughout this time, the hut was beginning to show its age, and with heavy rains, part of the ceiling crashed down! We rescued a lot of still-relevant material: books, journals, slides from our presentations, etc. These were secured in a portakabin located adjacent to the hut, and became the 'nerve centre' of our continuing work. It was a sad day when we finally had to say goodbye to our beloved hut.

The Rigours and Romance of a Database

As a medical student, I knew little about 'databases', a word I was unaware of at that time. The Medical Records Department at The Christian Medical College Hospital (CMCH) was good and made case records available to consultants for morbidity and mortality review. This ensured that discussions on outcomes were based on fact, from which much could be learnt, including ways to improve results.

At the time, I was busy learning the details about *individual* patients under my boss's care as I rotated through the medical and surgical units and the departments of obstetrics and gynaecology.

The public health and rural medicine programme, however, was different as the patients were widely scattered geographically. Nevertheless, one of our paediatricians had a major research interest in the relationship between consanguinity and clinical problems.

I became a registered doctor in 1964. Instinctively I sensed that databases might yield information as important as 'high-tech' medicine. With maturity came the realisation that a database is important as it is an 'inventory' of information. As to the methods of collecting the material and developing a database which could be repeatedly mined for knowledge – that was some years ahead!

Tummy, groans, guts and - - beyond!

When I became a consultant, my main area of clinical and research interest was in ulcer disease, so we developed a database devoted to this condition. The items recorded were names of patients, gender, date of birth, endoscopy findings and treatment: specifically, the drug used and the duration of treatment until the next review. Later, we were referred to an increasing number of patients with acid reflux, so we developed a specific database for such patients using the model for ulcer disease.

Patients with other gastrointestinal conditions, such as pancreatic problems, were limited in number, so we retained their information in master lists. The amount of information we gathered was the principal determinant of whether to develop a database or store it as a master list.

In my early days, Rotherham Hospital was a place medical students and young doctors wanted to avoid as they felt the training was not as good as in other centres. I was keen on teaching medical students even when I was a young doctor at my medical school, so I carried this habit over. Gradually, more students and young doctors preparing for higher examinations started to attend. So, the need for patients with 'interesting' clinical features grew. I used to jot names down in a pocket notebook, which my then-secretary started to record on index cards, the beginning of an informal database. Thus began the era of index cards - 'computer' was just a word I had heard about at Oxford when nearing the end of my research. At Rotherham, it was still a distant dream!

I must emphasise that in my early days, all physicians were regarded as 'general physicians' who would take care of patients with a variety of medical problems. As I was very inexperienced, this provided a wonderful learning opportunity.

I had interesting discussions with several medical students and young doctors. It was a wonderful time, and I could not get enough of it! I also learnt much from my senior consultant colleagues, some of whom had appointed me. I realised I could also learn a great deal from the patients, irrespective of their medical problems. As activity in Rotherham rapidly increased, more students and doctors were encouraged to have some of their training here. In those early days, I also had to cover the Montagu Hospital at Mexborough, about ten miles away. This provided a further venue for teaching and training.

Belatedly, I learnt the obvious! It is one thing if a patient is already on the ward and likely to be there for several days or longer, allowing the students, junior doctors and me time to learn from them. If, however, a patient with, say, a pleural effusion (fluid around the lung) is admitted, they are quite likely to be discharged shortly after the fluid is drained. The person may be willing to return specifically for a student teaching session, so there was the need to have a record to which further information could be added.

Looking back after all these many years, I suppose the databases we developed were 'instinctive', in response to a need 'sensed' – as opposed to being fully articulated! In effect, an evolutionary process of 'trial and error'. Some medical students wondered why, if Rotherham could provide interactions with patients regularly, i.e. teaching, other centres could not do so!

Several people were surprised to learn of our simple, indeed 'primitive', system. The fact is that a simple system, used consistently, can be productive!

Peptic ulcer

My main area of specific clinical and research interest was in peptic ulcer, duodenal ulcer (DU) in particular. This developed during my internship at CMCH, where peptic ulcer disease, particularly DU, was rife. The influence of a charismatic consultant physician in Vellore and some of the senior surgeons got me interested in this condition.

As a young consultant, I got increasingly intrigued about whether continued medical treatment with cimetidine would suffice or if early surgery would be a better option. I also tried the effect of increasing the dose of cimetidine to reduce the need for operation. It worked!

Thus, we worked using a combination of databases and master lists. This worked well for the gastroenterology team, developments funded by collaborative research with the pharmaceutical industry, and funds and second-hand equipment given to us by generous donors.

Our team regularly reviewed results to assess patient outcomes, check for gaps and errors, and discuss how we could improve. In effect, we were 'auditing' our performance for clinical and research needs - even before I had heard of the word 'audit'! I cannot remember when or why the clinical performance of individual doctors and team members became mandatory, but I recall the official 'training sessions' were preaching to the converted!

Experience taught me two things. First, I was poor at doing anything systematically, not least because I was erratic. In contrast, our team members were excellent as they had the necessary common-sense and judgement that I lacked!

Developing a useful database and maintaining high quality is a team effort, with every member having something to contribute. The databases we developed could be examined from different points of view, from which more information could be gleaned, as exemplified by the reference below.[13]

Radiology was the principal means of diagnosis, which over time gave way to gastroscopy as it allowed a far better view. Cimetidine, the first histamine H2 receptor antagonist (H2RA), reduced acid secretion considerably, thereby relieving pain and hastening ulcer healing. The increasing number of patients we saw was 'straining the system'. I was not persuaded, however, by the expert 'consensus' that endoscopic follow-up was unnecessary – which sounds arrogant as I was young and inexperienced. The reason for continued follow-up was that we had started to recognise

---

[13] Adam, Eve and the reflux enigma: age and gender differences across the gastro-oesophageal reflux spectrum. C Royston, KD Bardhan. *European Journal of Gastroenterology & Hepatology* 2017;29(6):634-9 doi:10.1097/MEG.0000000000000845

the entities of 'silent' DU (active disease but without symptoms) and 'refractory' DU (when the standard dose of Cimetidine proved insufficient). I was teased for being an "enthusiast", more focused on the procedure than its value! 'Good fortune' stepped in, as our team was able to present our emerging work at various national and international meetings, followed by publications which made our results available worldwide. This was possible because of the emerging strength of our growing database, characterised by the quantity and quality of information.

From peptic ulcer to other gastrointestinal disorders

Using the ulcer model, we developed databases covering the other areas in which we had a growing interest, specifically inflammatory bowel disease (IBD). We had a limited number of such patients, so the information was held as a 'master list'. My surgical consultant colleagues then asked me to look after their IBD patients and to refer back only if I felt an operation might be required. I thought they would have only a few patients under their care, but, to my astonishment, there was a large number! As new treatments started to emerge, our team's involvement grew. Specialist IBD nurses were appointed, and this increased the range of our activities. The nurse was the person the patient could contact directly in the event of problems, and she, in turn, would alert our medical staff. In view of the growing activity, we gradually converted the master list to a full database.

Database requirements

Through experience, our team learnt that the following features are important:

- Clear purpose

- Clarity of information: what needs to be included and what does not

- Flexibility, for example, adding information retrospectively
- When a new interest emerged, we began with a master list and developed a database only when our increasing activity made it necessary

As mentioned earlier, I recognised that our team members had far more to offer than I did!

At times such activity seemed impossibly large, but through discussion and cooperation, we developed a robust system which added valuable information and gave confidence to the patients.

For me, the greatest lesson I learnt was that others, specifically our team members, were more capable than I was of transforming 'dreams' into the direction and from there to reality, as their judgement was often better.

The flexibility and quality of our databases attracted attention from doctors in other specialities. We were happy to discuss the matter and were often asked for advice on their presentations. A point we repeatedly stressed was not to overload slides with dense tables but instead to simplify by highlighting the relevant features. Many of the youngsters were skilled with PowerPoint. I learnt the basics from family and friends and began understanding that a picture is worth more than many words. The problem was that I had only a vague idea of what I wanted and struggled to put it into words! As usual, I acted first – and only then began to think how best to record the information!

After the creation of a database for upper GI disorders, similar ones followed:

- Lower GI disorders (the numbers steadily rising)
- Other GI disorders, e.g. liver and pancreatic problems
- Non-GI problems, i.e. the rest of general medicine!

As usual, I had acted by instinct, later considering whether a database for non-GI problems would keep me away from gastroenterology. Yet time showed that observations made in 'general medicine' sometimes had a major impact on gastroenterology, for example, the recognition of superior mesenteric artery (SMA) stenosis, a rarity, from which arose studies on gut blood flow, and produced several very good PhDs.

We also noted patients with GI problems whom I discharged from follow-up as there was little further I could do to help at that time – but I could invite them back if suitable investigations and therapy became available.

A good example is troublesome unexplained diarrhoea - usually labelled 'irritable bowel syndrome' (IBS). The development of the SeHCAT retention test allowed recognition of bile acid malabsorption (BAM), later re-labelled by experts as bile acid diarrhoea (BAD). Treatment with bile salt sequestrants greatly changed the lives of many.

Many contributed to the development of the databases over the years, both at Rotherham and at Montagu Hospital at Mexborough: scribbled notes on scraps of paper and in notebooks became an alphabetical card index system. The principal contributors were Beverley Mason, Christine Royston, Liz Mott and Christine Roddis, based at Rotherham.

Chandu's 'angels': Bev, Liz & Christine

A computerised system was later set up by our first PhD student shortly before the development of IT systems within the hospital. This was not for his PhD but would allow Christine Roddis to maintain a list of publications she and Mr Ishaque had gathered. Christine Royston then joined our team and transferred the information from the card index system to the computer. The machine was slow to generate the required information but far quicker than a manual search. The computer systems went through a series of steps using the hardware and software available, increasing the capacity to store information and retrieve it quickly.

Bob, our first PhD student

We were rapidly gathering a lot of data. We learnt that the quantity of data alone is insufficient: it requires quality; the hardest part was maintaining consistency over a long period, sometimes for a patient's lifetime. It is maintaining a consistently high quality that deters many.

Maintaining a high-quality database is not a short sprint but more of a marathon, as it needs constant updating. For us, this was made possible by Bev Mason, my secretary, and Christine Royston, supported by other close colleagues and nurses funded by the family research charity we had created, The Bardhan Research & Education Trust of Rotherham (BRET).

Information from our databases has supported several multicentre therapeutic trials. An example is the inflammatory bowel disease (IBD) study initiated by a major pharmaceutical company. Their representatives visited many centres, the plan being to produce a nationwide database, generating reports based upon several thousands of patients as opposed to just a few hundred or fewer in previous years. A special attraction was being able to report on long-term clinical progress and outcome.

We submitted a paper and the referee rightly pointed out that set against the ambitious aim, the report was based on data from just a handful of centres, including ours. I phoned the editor in sorrow but, from the heart, confessed that despite initial enthusiasm, the heavy clinical duties of a consultant made it difficult for some to continue their involvement.

Databases for teaching and training medical students and junior doctors

As the number of referrals from GPs and consultants increased, I saw patients with a wide variety of conditions. Gradually the type of data increased, from X-rays showing specific features to changes in blood counts.

When students and junior doctors made additional observations or questioned me on specific points, I would be reminded of the aphorism, 'for as we teach, so we learn' - how very true.

The patients would sometimes join in! On one occasion, an elderly gentleman told me, "It's good to see you training the youngsters" – recounting his time in the military, where he had good trainers. On other occasions, patients gave tips on how to get the point across more effectively!

Teaching and training

We used a similar approach to create a database of patients who had kindly volunteered to participate in our teaching programme for medical students and junior doctors, which the recipients greatly appreciated. Our Department of Medical Education and Training steadily grew, staffed by very capable people. Sheffield University medical students were placed in various hospitals in the region.

Their feedback indicated that Rotherham was highly regarded as a training centre.

Let me illustrate this with a few examples.

Upper gastrointestinal haemorrhage (UGIH)

UGIH from peptic ulcer disease remained a problem for many years. When severe, it would require surgery to stop the bleeding (haemostasis), with or without a definitive operation to cure the ulcer. Mortality remained at about ten per cent.

The expansion of diagnostic gastroscopy was soon followed by endoscopic means of stopping haemorrhage, for example, injecting the ulcer base with adrenaline, with or without a sclerosing agent (which closes the vessel by 'gumming it up'). Later, cautery was added, heat-sealing the vessel, and further development was to apply a clip to the vessel, which would close it.

From such databases, the Rockall Score and the Glasgow Blatchford Score were developed to predict the likely outcome.

We participated in the national audit programme and established a dedicated hotline for clinicians to let us know whenever a patient was admitted with bleeding. It did not matter if the calls were duplicated: what *did* matter was not doing so, assuming another staff member may already have phoned! Christine Royston, Bev and I repeatedly emphasised this message to new staff when they joined. The results were reported in several publications, including the major one shown below.[14]

---

[14] Incidence of and mortality from acute upper gastrointestinal haemorrhage in the United Kingdom. TA Rockall, FRA Logan, HB Devlin, TC Northfield on behalf of the Steering Committee & members of the National Audit of Acute Upper Gastrointestinal Haemorrhage. *British Medical Journal* 1995;311:222-6

The UK Barrett's Oesophagus Registry

The gullet (oesophagus) is lined by cells resembling skin (minus hairs!). Acid reflux, when excessive, irritates the lining of the gullet and causes symptoms such as heartburn and regurgitation. Another consequence of reflux is that the gullet lining changes, resembling that of the stomach and, more often, the gut. Barrett's oesophagus is named after Dr Norman Rupert Barrett, who felt that this was a manifestation of a short gullet. The importance of its recognition is that Barrett's dysplasia is a pre-cancerous condition. It was only later that I learnt that the gullet lining could be damaged without any visible signs.

Once again, many centres joined, but only a handful sustained the effort. Hence to extract data, the Rotherham database was repeatedly 'mined' because of its quality. Amongst other things, we learnt the incidence of Barrett's was rising at Rotherham, so it was likely more would ultimately develop oesophageal cancer.

We had earlier recognised an association between blood groups and *Helicobacter pylori* infection.[15]

We now recognised a strong association between Barrett's oesophagus and those with blood group O who were also Rhesus negative. A persuasive case had been put forward that nitrates from the soil in foodstuffs are repeatedly re-circulated and re-secreted through the parotid salivary glands (which are located at the angle of the jaw). Such nitrates are potentially carcinogenic. At this point, I was lost as I could not see any mechanism which could cause this. When our family from the USA visited, my son-in-law took the time to review the data and worked out a mechanism by which

---

[15] (The seroprevalence of *Helicobacter pylori* in UK blood donors - A story of town and country. D Morton, RJ Sokol, MA Chapman, KD Bardhan. *Gut* 1998;42 (Suppl 1):A77 (TF307)

oesophageal cancer could arise. To great delight, the team insisted on including him as a co-author.[16]

The Adam and Eve hypothesis paper

Barrett's oesophagus affects men predominantly, as does gullet cancer. I was aware that ischaemic heart disease affects men predominantly, whereas women seem protected during their reproductive life. The Guardian's science correspondent drew attention to a report in The New Scientist that such protection is true for a range of other disorders.

Christine Royston and I reflected on the matter for some weeks and, digging deeper, found evidence that men's saliva is unchanging in its acid-neutralising capacity. In contrast, women's saliva varies with the menstrual cycle. We then unearthed a reference in a Japanese journal that there are specialised cells in the salivary gland which mediate this effect. The American Gastroenterological Association accepted our poster for presentation at the annual Digestive Disease Week: 'Adam, Eve and Barrett's enigma' – which attracted quite a lot of attention, partly because of the unusual title.

So we took it further and developed a full paper, which Christine Royston submitted one Friday evening in early December 2016. The journal editor looked at it the next day and sent an E-mail stating that our report had been accepted and that no changes were necessary. This is the first time that a database paper has been accepted like this. We wrote to the editor to thank him, adding that Santa Claus really exists and this year had come early!

Developing a good database is hard work but maintaining it is even harder and requires stamina. Christine Royston and Bev,

---

[16] Barrett's, blood groups and progression to oesophageal cancer: is nitric oxide the link? CPJ Caygill, C Royston, A Charlett, CM Wall, PAC Gatenby, JR Ramus, A Watson, M Winslet, CS Hourigan, KD Bardhan. *European Journal of Gastroenterology & Hepatology* 2011;23(9):801-6 doi: 10.1097/MEG.0b013e3283489dcf

together with some of their colleagues, made an outstanding team that patients admired as we followed up on their progress, often phoning them to check how they were getting on.

One finds that with good people, hard work is a pleasure. Benefits often follow, some ground-breaking and leading to research degrees such as Masters, PhDs and MDs.

"Lies, damned lies, and statistics" – in a whisper!

I was summoned by the Chief Executive to be told that amongst all the physicians, my patients had the longest length of in-patent stay. This surprised me, but I did not have the time to investigate further. So the Chief Executive kindly approached Sheffield Hallam University, and they sent a young man to help us. A patient in his 40s was identified: he had survived a severe stroke but was not well enough to be discharged home nor old enough to be transferred to the Department for Elderly Medicine – a real 'Catch 22' problem! The incident changed the life of the youngster from Sheffield Hallam University, who was drawn to a career in hospital administration.

Looking back in retirement, I can honestly say it has been a wonderful journey.

Bile Acids and the Small Intestine: Foe --- or Friend?

Background

Since my early days at Rotherham, the 'natural home' of our clinical research was in the field of peptic ulcer and acid reflux disease, later expanding to include inflammatory bowel disease and pancreatic insufficiency.

As a houseman at Hammersmith Hospital in London, I had been aware of the entity 'bile acid malabsorption' (BAM). Keen to learn more, I approached the scientists there who were working in this area. They were sympathetic but stressed that this was a specialist field and they did not have the time to teach me.

At Rotherham Hospital, I had the opportunity to work closely with our wonderful department of Medical Physics. The Head of the department drew my attention to the SeHCAT retention test, a simple, non-invasive means of recognising BAM. Traditionally, patients had to collect their faeces for three to five days, and the amount of bile acids passed was measured, a long process not always pleasant. In contrast, the SeHCAT retention test does not require any sample collection, which is a great relief!

The acronym SeHCAT is an abbreviation of tauroselcholic ^{75}selenium acid, a bile salt tagged with a tiny dose of radioactive selenium. The patient swallows a capsule containing the radioactive isotope then lies on a couch which travels up until the patient's body is under the counter. A baseline count is then measured. The patient returns a week later for a repeat count. Retention of less than ten per cent is abnormal. The simplicity of the test resulted in our investigation of a large number of patients. So we were able to help many with treatment using bile acid sequestrants, a class of drugs which binds unabsorbed bile acids, thereby easing or preventing diarrhoea.

Our results were reported in the Journal of The Royal College of Physicians of London (Vol 43, No. 5, Sept/Oct 2000). I was invited to present a State of the Art lecture at the British Society of Gastroenterology meeting in Birmingham on Tuesday, 21 March 2006. The invitation came in late 2005, just before I went to Cape Town on a short sabbatical, so whilst there, I had time to reflect and assemble my thoughts.

On returning to Rotherham, I had to make up for lost time, and in addition to my daily clinical work, my life became taken over by the presentation. Every evening was spent working on this lecture, resuming very early in the mornings before heading off to the hospital. In effect, my habit of driving everyone crazy reached a peak! My former trainee and successor maintained tight editorial control as he was well aware of my habit of not knowing when to stop!

Whilst at the gym, I listened to the science podcast 'Life on Earth', and it was then that the moment of inspiration came to start my presentation from an evolutionary viewpoint.

I sought the advice of the Professor of Organic Chemistry at The University of Sheffield. He gave me several personal tutorials and conducted experiments to show the nature of emulsification.

At the end, I acknowledged and thanked the many who had made this presentation possible. In total, one hundred and eleven slides were shown. Most would say this was far too many for a one-hour lecture. However, the slides 'evolved': one brief line of text at a time, to which other text in different colours and images were added. Therefore, I could speak at a steady rate, finishing with a few minutes to spare!

Thankfully the presentation went well, the product of endless preparation and rehearsals. The chairman graciously remarked that it had been one of the best State of the Art lectures. I am grateful to the many who forgave my habit of constantly pestering them – but it was worth it, for I did not let down 'Team Rotherham'!

To our surprise, we also identified patients who presented with irritable bowel syndrome (IBS) symptoms and had an intact gastrointestinal tract yet had BAM/BAD. The proportion was small, but the group as a whole was very large. So it is worthwhile investigating such patients. If they have BAM/BAD, their symptoms could be relieved by a class of drugs called bile acid sequestrants. The reason is that bile acids not absorbed in the terminal ileum spill into the colon, where they trigger diarrhoea.

SeHCAT proved a very useful tool for recognising those whose diarrhoea could be attributed to bile acid malabsorption. As mentioned earlier, patients can be offered treatment with bile acid sequestrants, designed to absorb the excess of bile acids in the gut. Cholestyramine was the standard drug but had an unpleasant taste. Flavouring helps, so we used Colestipol Orange, which is much more palatable. An added advantage is that the powder can be dissolved in water, and a day's supply can be taken in portions, the unused part being kept in a refrigerator. In effect, the patients titrate their own dose.

My team and I owe much to our patients as we have learnt a lot from their insights. One person, in particular, comes to mind. A soccer fanatic, he could no longer attend matches because of diarrhoea which could erupt suddenly. Since going on to treatment, he could go out without fear of diarrhoea and resume attending soccer matches, which was a great joy for him. He and many other patients at the receiving end of treatment have taught me a great deal, and I am very grateful to them.

Some Interesting Patients' Stories

Sick as a parrot – Masquerade!

The young man was desperately ill: breathless, lips blue despite the high concentration of oxygen delivered through his facemask, which almost concealed sunken eyes, his paleness contrasting with his striking ginger hair.

The pneumonia did not respond to any of the antibiotics we tried in increasing desperation. Legionnaires' disease had been described recently, but we could not prove its presence. Then quite suddenly, he suffered a heart attack, and to me, it seemed only a matter of time, a day or two at most and perhaps only hours, between the 'now' and 'the beyond'.

Whilst he was on the Coronary Care Unit it transpired that he kept a parrot. I cannot remember from where we got this information, but it was highly relevant as parrots and many other birds often harbour an organism of the class *Chlamydia psittaci*. The microbe that causes this illness is common in birds and poultry, but often it does not trouble the bird. Humans, however, can inhale the organism, usually from airborne particles from a bird's faeces or feathers, and develop pneumonia as a result.

I was informed that three specialists were travelling to Rotherham to advise and help, but my relief turned to dismay on learning that they would be attending to the parrot, not the patient! They took blood samples from its heart to ensure enough was available for the different tests, but unfortunately, the parrot was killed in the process!

The National Centre of Infectious Disease Surveillance and Control is based at Colindale Avenue in London. The centre closely monitors all notifiable diseases, studies their patterns, and alerts all microbiologists. Accordingly, our own microbiologist, with whom

I had worked for many years, was notified of its surprising new finding. In laboratory tests, a cross-reaction was detected between the organism causing psittacosis and the one responsible for Legionnaires' disease, the implication being that Legionnaires' may be masquerading as psittacosis.

We immediately changed the antibiotics to the ones more effective against *Legionella pneumophila*, the bug causing Legionnaires' disease. Lo and behold! Our patient started to improve; for this, he, my team and I were truly thankful.

I saw the patient years later at Tesco Extra in the town centre, and we recognised each other immediately. He was using his shopping trolley as much for physical support as for carrying his purchases. The day was warm, yet his lips started to turn blue (cyanosis) when he spoke. The reason for cyanosis is that the lungs have a lot of blood and air, but these are not distributed in perfect balance. When upright, more air is at the top of the lungs, with more blood in the lower parts. This phenomenon is technically termed 'ventilation-perfusion imbalance'. In healthy people, the imbalance is only small; it neither reduces physical performance nor causes changes in appearance. When there is lung disease, the mismatch increases; this reduces physical performance, with the lips turning blue during any effort, even walking slowly. So this poor patient was left with residual problems.

When I meet former patients, it is for me 'special'. When a patient has survived against all the odds, the meeting is 'joyous' and truly humbling, and I feel eternally grateful for having been blessed with the opportunity to be of some help.

The microbe causing Legionnaire's disease is widespread. It can be found in rivers, but free-flowing water is too cold to allow it to grow. The danger arises when the water is in heating systems, as the organisms multiply at 18°C to 60°C.

Gems of information

The course of an individual's illness is often guided by information which emerges only later. Delay occurs because of failures to seek relevant information, for example, recent overseas travel in someone with fever or diarrhoea. A further twist occurs when the person may have been treated overseas but cannot remember the names of medications used, whether prescribed or purchased over the counter. Occasionally, information is deliberately concealed, for example, excessive alcohol, which can lead to disasters.

One variant is when information emerges, but no one can quite remember how it came about, as in the case of my patient. Nevertheless, it proved crucial and helped the patient to turn the corner. The organism had been recognised some time earlier, but its virulence was unknown until the outbreak in Philadelphia. The American Legion had met for their annual convention at a hotel before returning to their homes, widely scattered throughout the USA. Many fell ill, and a high proportion died; this was revealed in national statistics as a sudden peak of pneumonia at an unexpected time, the striking feature being the high death rate.

The standard epidemiological approach to such outbreaks is 'Time, Place and Person'. The time span was probably narrow, within days or weeks of the convention, the common factor being that the people affected had gathered at the same place.

Quite by chance, I had attended a gastroenterology meeting in the USA to make a presentation and had returned home from Philadelphia. I could not resist asking my host about the Legionella outbreak. He kindly drove me past the hotel, which was now in a sorry state, poorly lit and unused, despite the outbreak having occurred several months earlier. I sensed that such 'bad news' about a once prosperous hotel lingers, so nobody wants to use it; as a result, management is understandably reluctant to spend large amounts of money to bring it back to its former state.

It would be different if the hotel were damaged by fire or flood, as these are tangible to the layperson, whereas Legionella is less so. Sad but true.

Mellow Yellow

Prelude: A new dawn!

As a medical student, I learnt that the body has complex, highly coordinated defence mechanisms to protect us from infections. Within this spectrum is the immune system, which distinguishes 'self' from 'non-self', i.e. that which is foreign and potentially dangerous and which the immune system will therefore attack and destroy.

My research area at Oxford was related to intrinsic factor (IF) and pernicious anaemia (PA). IF is a substance secreted by the parietal cells lining the stomach, which also secrete acid. Vitamin B12 is scarce in the diet; hence IF harvests the entire available vitamin. However, in PA, a major change occurs such that the immune system no longer recognises the stomach lining with which it earlier lived in harmony. It therefore launches an attack which ultimately deprives the person of both IF and acid. This state renders the stomach more likely to develop cancer.

I was not able to foresee that a dysfunctional immune system might target other parts of the body, specifically the thyroid gland and the pancreas!

The era of raw liver for the treatment of pernicious anaemia was followed by the phase where patients were treated with scrapings from pigs' stomachs, which are rich in intrinsic factor. Being foreign, the defence system would react accordingly, which could be shown in the laboratory. One of the scientists in the Nuffield Department of Medicine kept a record of all patients treated; he noted that one patient tested positive yet had never been treated with hog stomach! This brilliant observation was a turning point. Why did this patient develop antibodies against IF? The pursuit for an answer led to the recognition that in PA the body's immune system attacks the stomach.

Quis custodiet ipsos custodes?

'Who guards the guards?' This phrase, I learnt, comes from the Roman poet Juvenal. In my mind, it captures the nature of autoimmune disorders.

As a medical student and junior doctor, I learnt that painless progressive jaundice usually signifies the presence of cancer within the head of the pancreas and is usually incurable.

Bile and pancreatic juice are essential for the efficient digestion and absorption of food. Both fluids are discharged into the second part of the duodenum, the exit guarded by a ring of muscle (a sphincter), which is regulated to open and close at the right time.

In contrast, the person who develops pain and then jaundice is much more likely to have gallstones blocking the bile duct, which during my early days was relieved by cholecystectomy (removal of the gallbladder by open surgery). Nowadays, stones are removed by an endoscopic procedure before a laparoscopic cholecystectomy, i.e. keyhole surgery.

'Stones' or 'something else'?

RJ is the patient who changed my views! I saw her in the mid-1980s when she was admitted with deepening jaundice and had dark urine and constant itching, characteristic of obstructive jaundice. The outlook was bad, but my senior surgical colleague wanted to relieve her symptoms; accordingly, he operated. The head of the pancreas was hard, as would be expected with cancer. In those days, the view was that trying to confirm the diagnosis by taking a biopsy could worsen matters as the pancreatic enzymes (digestive ferments) would leak out and cause further damage.

Instead, he carried out a bypass operation (gastrojejunostomy) whereby the stomach is detached from the duodenum (the first part of the small gut) and reconnected further down to the jejunum (the second part). The new connection was wide, deliberately so, to allow the easy passage of food.

To my surprise, jaundice faded! The patient steadily improved and regained energy and weight! Her only problem now was bloating and "wind", but the Head Pharmacist could not recommend any effective remedy.

I then recalled my student days when I was afflicted with diarrhoea and weight loss caused by the parasite *Giardia lamblia*. I could not tolerate Mepacrine, the recommended treatment, as it made me ill. My father came to the rescue with a simple but effective treatment: wood charcoal! It absorbs gas, the same principle used in gasmasks. The only slight drawback was a temporarily blackened mouth, but in my case, this was not a problem as the charcoal tasted rather nice!

RJ was horrified when I suggested this treatment! The surgeon was getting used to my eccentric ways and supported me. Our Consultant Biochemist and the Head Pharmacist came to the rescue when they identified Carbellon, a tablet made from a charcoal derivative, and obtained a small supply. RJ found it effective, even pleasant, and this was a relief.

To this day, more than 30 years on, RJ remains well. Her son is a porter at our hospital; I see him from time to time and ask about his mother, and she always passes on her good wishes.

'Fate' came knocking again!

A GP contacted me requesting an urgent domiciliary consultation. The patient, CS, had given birth three weeks earlier and since then had noticed progressive deepening jaundice: dark urine, yellow eyes and yellow skin, along with intense itching. Strikingly, she had *no* pain. As with RJ, I felt she had cancer in the head of the pancreas, which her GP suspected. The surgeon concurred and operated urgently, finding a hard mass in the head of the pancreas and bypassing it by creating a gastrojejunostomy (as with patient RJ). The surgeon could see I was upset as CS was a young mother. He told me gently that such tragic events happen in medicine and, sadly, she would soon pass away.

She was referred to my outpatient clinic many years later, to my pleasant surprise! Far from passing away, she had put on weight and indeed joked about having something done to reverse this! Her main problem now was a cough, breathlessness, loose stools, and sometimes diarrhoea. Her GP referred her, knowing I would be pleased to see her again, particularly as I had written that she would soon pass away! I discussed her problems with our chest physician: he suspected the underlying problem might be fibrosing alveolitis, a lung condition caused by exposure to various substances, including fungal spores. I wondered if autoimmune damage might play a part, but there was no clear evidence.

A fortunate meeting

Whilst at a major gastroenterology meeting in the USA, I met my former trainee and friend, who introduced me to one of his colleagues based at The Mayo Clinic, an expert on autoimmune pancreatitis (AIP). He gave a lecture on the subject. The disease pattern he described was very similar to that of our two patients. This was encouraging and strengthened my view that CS fell into the clinical spectrum of AIP. I could not, however, exclude the possibility of another autoimmune disease process that had contributed to her symptoms.

Back at Rotherham, I decided to check CS for coeliac disease, which by now was well known to be triggered by wheat. Its diagnosis is made by checking the appearance of biopsies taken from the small intestine. A healthy small gut is lined by villi, finger-like delicate projections. In those days, such biopsies were obtained using a Crosby capsule, a mechanical device tethered to a long tube, which the patient swallowed. Once in the stomach, the capsule was guided into the duodenum and, if possible, advanced further down the small intestine. This long, drawn-out, tedious process was sometimes worsened when the capsule would not work!

In the case of CS, however, it was particularly easy as the difficult parts to get around had been surgically bypassed, and I could reach fairly far down the small intestine! The mucosal biopsies showed that the villi were stunted, flat or lost altogether. Such a pattern is typical of coeliac disease, an immune-mediated condition related to the presence of gluten, a crucial component of wheat germ.

The treatment is a gluten-free diet. So our dietician started CS on this regime, and she blossomed into health once again.

I was intrigued that autoimmune damage had affected the digestive system in two places: a solid structure, the pancreas, and a hollow one, the small intestine. I wondered how many other patients under my care might have been affected in a similar manner.

Later, CS had to undergo a hysterectomy and oophorectomy, i.e. removal of the uterus and the ovaries. I requested the pathologist to examine the resected specimens for signs of autoimmune damage, for example, infiltration of immune cells into the ovaries and the endometrium, the lining of the uterus. He was, however, fed up with my endless enquiries and told me to buzz off!

Through experience, I realised that every patient allows us to learn. When diagnosis and treatment are successful, we consolidate knowledge. New avenues open up for exploration, sometimes with the patient as an active participant!

A Peaceful Passing

In the mid-1990s at Rotherham Endoscopy Unit

I sedated the patient and passed the gastroscope into her stomach. On looking up at the video screen, I was surprised to see a large ulcerating stomach cancer, its very size suggesting it was probably incurable. The abdomen was relaxed, so I could easily feel any abnormality. The liver was huge, and in these circumstances was probably because the cancer had spread. The sister-in-charge kindly phoned the Radiology Department to arrange for an urgent ultrasound examination. This confirmed metastases, suggesting the inevitable outcome.

The finality of the situation appalled me as the lady was only middle-aged with mild symptoms which had not fully settled on acid-suppressing medication. Her GP, based at Doncaster, was one of my former medical students who later became a house officer on our team. She had clearly benefited from the experience as she wisely referred her patient for gastroscopy instead of disregarding the mild symptoms.

The effects of sedation faded in a couple of hours. The patient, her husband, the endoscopy sister, and I gathered in the nearby consulting room. I discussed the diagnosis and, importantly, the outlook, which in her case amounted to a matter of a few months at most. Far from breaking down, she remained the picture of calm composure.

I asked her what her dearest wish was in the limited time she had. She and her husband set their hearts on going to Australia to see family and grandchildren, which would be the last time for her in these circumstances. I prescribed powerful morphine-based painkillers.

I phoned my secretary, and she promptly came to the Endoscopy Unit. I began dictating the letter in front of everyone so that the patient and her husband could add comments. Bev swiftly typed the letter and brought it back to the Unit. I advised the husband to carry a copy with him at all times so that if his wife needed medical help on the journey or when in Australia, all details were at hand.

Their trip to Australia was to be a month. Some weeks after the consultation, I received a phone call from her husband, who told me they had had a wonderful and loving reunion with the family and grandchildren, emphasizing that she had not required morphine. Tired after the long journey, they went home, and during the night, she passed away in her sleep, her final wish granted. I was profoundly moved and thanked him for having kept me informed.

The following week, the Endoscopy Sister phoned me in my office and told me I had some visitors at the Unit who wanted to see me. They turned out to be the lady's husband, the referring GP and her medical colleague, who had been greatly moved by the sequence of events.

Prescribing powerful analgesics for someone with a malignant disease going away on a long journey has medico-legal risks. Some months earlier, I faced a similar situation after confirming an incurable malignant condition in a Chinese lady in her 60s. I discussed the issues with her daughter, who explained that her mother's final wish was to die in China. The daughter then asked for powerful painkillers to help her mother on the long flight and to ease her final days. I fully sympathised with her request but sensed there might be medico-legal issues. I consulted The Medical Protection Society (of which I am a member), who advised that prescribing powerful painkillers for somebody leaving Britain was contentious, regardless of its intended good.

So, I asked the daughter to give me a few hours to reflect. I concluded that in these circumstances, I felt that giving powerful painkillers was the right thing to do.

The moral purpose of medicine is paramount and brings to mind a statement attributed to Hippocrates (460-370 BC). He made many important observations on the practice of medicine and how doctors should conduct themselves. One of these appealed to me as, despite the major advances in medicine, it remains true even today: "Cure sometimes, relieve often, comfort always". These days we are able to cure many more people, but sometimes, it is beyond us.

So then, one has to treat others as best as one can. We will always be faced with people for whom we cannot do much, but to me, humanity demands "comfort always". For that reason, when it came to the lady from Doncaster, I had no hesitation in prescribing the painkillers.

Success: Illusion & Reality

1993: Operation Theatre 6 at Rotherham General Hospital

We reviewed the instructional video several times, and the dummy runs were over. Today was 'the real thing', the first time we had ever attempted the novel technique of percutaneous endoscopic gastrostomy for artificial feeding, usually referred to simply as PEG.

With theatre lights dimmed, we found ourselves speaking in hushed voices! Assisting me were our endoscopy nurses and Registrar, the very capable middle-grade trainee.

The patient, rendered incapable of swallowing because of his stroke, was sedated, sleeping and breathing quietly. I had the gastroscope inside his stomach, its tip glowing ghost-like in the surrounding darkness like a Halloween lantern. The Registrar 'prodded' the lit area of the abdomen with his index finger whilst I observed the stomach from the inside. It was amazing to see the inner surface now indented. "Well done", I exclaimed, "Just try a few more jiggles." The moment he got his finger aligned to form a right-angled indent, I said it was perfect and to hold still. "Is it OK to breathe?" the Registrar asked, easing the tension!

He injected Lignocaine, a local anaesthetic, where he had indented the tummy and deep into the tissues to ensure the whole area was numb. Next, he made a small incision and passed the trocar, a hollow wide bore device the width of a knitting needle, until it punctured the stomach wall. After I could see the trocar tip, the Registrar and I worked together in coordinated steps. He passed a wire with a loop at its end through the trocar; I guided closed biopsy forceps through the one-metre length of the gastroscope into the stomach, opened its jaws, grasped the wire loop and pulled. There was gentle resistance at first, as expected. I pulled again, and out popped a silicone-coated rubber tube the width of a pencil. One last pull and the restraining flange, shaped like a large button, came through. I pulled the button up snugly against the stomach wall and taped the other end of the tube to the skin.

We were now ready to start feeding our patient with liquidised high-energy food, all the goodness of real 'nosh' and in large amounts. This was necessary to maintain daily needs and build up the body reserves depleted earlier.

As an aside, roughly three-quarters of our daily energy intake is used simply to keep us alive; the remainder is expended on physical work, such as getting about.

Somewhat confusingly, the movement of the hand or leg is controlled by the *opposite* side of the brain. The centres which control speech *and* swallowing are located in the lower left brain. So when a stroke damages this area, the patient often has difficulty swallowing.

A temporary alternative route of feeding is a nasogastric tube. A thin tube is passed through the nostril and guided down the gullet into the stomach. This helps but only for limited periods, as otherwise, the tube damages the gullet. Intravenous feeding is the alternative, a major advance but carrying unavoidable risks, the principal danger being infection tracking along the plastic tubing into the bloodstream.

Our patient was being fed intravenously, but because of vein access problems, we considered him suitable for PEG feeding. To my embarrassment, I had forgotten to liaise with the Pharmacy nutrition team! They turned up with large bags of prepared intravenous nutrition only to be greeted by a patient with a strange device taped to his stomach! This resulted in a lot of red medical faces. But the team really got into the spirit of things, and soon PEG feeding became established.

I had assumed PEG feeding would be required only occasionally. Surprisingly, however, the initial trickle of referrals grew into a torrent.

I had learnt from experience that patients' outcomes are not uncommonly at variance with what is expected. So we ensured that all our patients were followed up by periodic review, by telephone if necessary. In parallel, my secretary refined and ran a remarkable 'flare-up' system which ensured that patients could contact us directly if concerns arose, without having to trouble their GP for re-referral.

In contrast, we found it difficult to get detailed information about PEG patients from the referring consultants. Once I had done the procedure, patients were transferred from the hospital to their own homes or nursing homes. Much of our work was financed by funds we raised through research. Our team was over-stretched, and we could not spare time to find out the details.

In 1996, the new Specialist Registrar joined my unit. He is a most remarkable young man, now a world authority on coeliac disease and nutritional matters and head of a large outstanding team. He has also written a wonderful book, 'Gluten Attack', which explains in plain language the mysteries and science behind coeliac disease and how to cope with it.

He was aware of my misgivings at the increasing number of patients being referred for PEG feeding and whether the patients were benefiting or otherwise. With extraordinary energy, working very long hours, he began to collect data at Rotherham. We used to meet in Sheffield at the home of his close friend. Printouts of results were spread out on the floor, and we began to extract the crucial information. My fears proved justified, and I will expand on this shortly. At the end of a year with me, he moved to Doncaster as part of his training. There too, they had experienced a marked increase in PEG referrals but had not had the time to review their results in detail.

This figure is from our *American Journal of Gastroenterology* paper published in 2000.[17] A 'life-table analysis' was done.

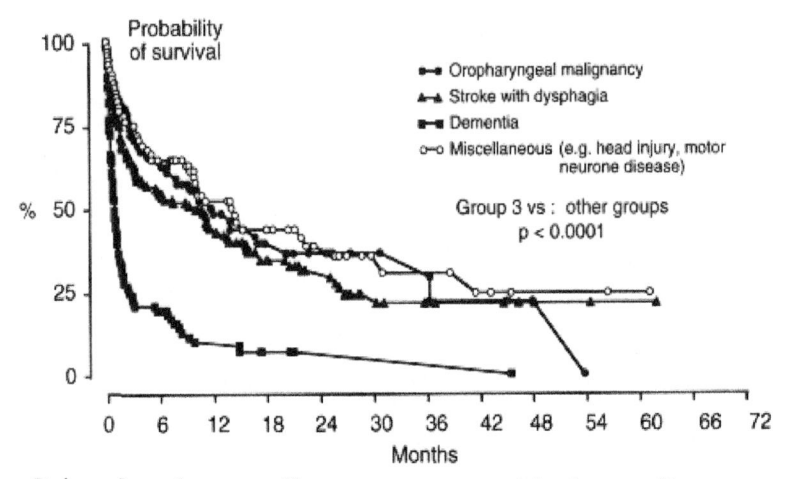

- It is a fact that we all must pass on to 'the beyond' at some stage. From middle age onwards, the path ahead gets shorter.

- It is similarly a fact that if already ill, no matter the cause, the chance of dying earlier is higher. The four groups bunched at the top of the figure all had serious problems, so it is not surprising to see a high death rate over the succeeding three to four years.

The bottom line, Group Three, represents the patients who were PEG-fed *not* because of any difficulty in swallowing but because of dementia. This condition can result in losing interest in food, being unaware of their surroundings and unable to look after themselves. Their mortality rate was calamitous. For all other PEG-fed patients,

---

[17] Survival Analysis in Percutaneous Endoscopic Gastrostomy Feeding: A Worse Outcome in Patients with Dementia. DS Sanders, MJ Carter, J D'Silva, G James, RP Bolton, and KD Bardhan (Vol. 95, No. 6, 2000)

the death rate at thirty days was twenty-eight per cent, but amongst those with dementia, fifty-four per cent were dead at one month and ninety per cent by one year.

I found these results disturbing. In medicine, we strive to help but recognise that not every treatment or intervention works out as we had hoped. I discussed the complexities with our hospital chaplain and a rehabilitation expert; furthermore, I convened a meeting of all medical and nursing staff involved with PEG. Our chaplain recognised the realities of bed shortage and that we medics have a duty to the hospital to discharge patients *safely* at the earliest opportunity. In addition, he pointed out that those in medicine have a responsibility to the patient, enshrined by the Hippocratic Oath; "First, do no harm". This complex area touches on human nature and morality and, in *my* view, represents a higher responsibility.

In 1998, we presented our results in New Orleans at the prestigious Digestive Diseases Week.[18] The presentation raised great interest, and in the interval, many American gastroenterologists shared their experiences. They were under pressure to start PEG feeding as it was more "cost-effective" than recruiting more staff to help feed a patient. Once the procedure was started, the patient could be discharged to a nursing home. Put differently; there were financial 'disincentives' to do otherwise.

This was sobering to hear and led to major changes in our practice. From then on, every patient referred was thoroughly assessed by the endoscopy nurses familiar with the procedure and aided by the gastroenterologists. Many patients would *not* benefit, and the number selected for PEG at Rotherham fell dramatically.

---

[18] Percutaneous endoscopic gastrostomy (PEG): The unseen mortality. D Sanders, MJ Carter, J D'Silva, G James, RP Bolton, KD Bardhan. American Gastroenterological Association: New Orleans, 17-20 May 1998

Our specialist registrar from 1996 had become a professor at Sheffield. Under his leadership, one of our former junior doctors investigated the outcome of such artificial feeding in detail and published the results in the international journal *Clinical Gastroenterology & Hepatology*. This was truly ground-breaking as it addressed quantitative as well as qualitative outcomes. 'Quantitative', as the name indicates, measures numbers. 'Qualitative', which deals with matters such as the quality of life, also has its own rigorous methodology.

He showed how technology had moved on; feeding tubes can now be placed under X-ray control instead of gastroscopy. He went on to grapple with the difficult task of examining the physical and psychological well-being of patients and caregivers and the social consequences of such artificial feeding.

The bottom line was that such artificial feeding did not always improve or help the patient. Nor did it necessarily help the family or caregivers. The concluding sentence is telling: "This work emphasises the importance of patient selection and the need to appropriately counsel patients and their care-givers before gastrostomy insertion". This self-evidently is common sense and underlines what we medics should be doing, you might say. The reality, however, is often different. For this ground-breaking work, he was awarded the degree of MD by the University of Sheffield.

I continue to learn and refine. 'Insight' is an important lesson as it forces me to pause for reflection and to consider how I can do better.

An extreme PEG

Our remarkable maxillofacial surgeon had asked me to carry out a PEG for a patient whose cancer had affected his upper jaw, resulting in the loss of an eye and severe scarring of his throat from irradiation. I wondered how to reach the gullet. The patient, a brave and charming man, duly took out his false eye, and I could go through the orbit into the gullet, hoping I would not be sick! The procedure went very well, much to everyone's delight. The head of our Medical Illustrations Department kindly took several photographs of the patient giving the thumbs-up sign surrounded by all the staff!

The British Science Association (BSA)

The BSA holds its annual science festival in September, a wonderful mind-stimulating event, thoroughly enjoyable and spread over three to four days. It is hosted at universities across the country, with many attendees being accommodated in the residence halls. A very wide range of subjects is covered by outstanding scientists who often feature regularly in TV and radio broadcasts and whose work is reported by newspapers.

Its prelude is the British Science Week in March. Events are organised for members of the public across the country, and, importantly, schoolchildren are encouraged to attend. Scientists speak to each other in their own language, which the layperson may not understand. Fortunately, some scientists are superb communicators and can express the 'magic' of their field to laymen, even to schoolchildren. One such person is Prof Charles Stirling - an outstanding example.

Prof Stirling encouraged me to make presentations at schools during science week. I spoke at several schools. At one school, there were several children from Somalia. The teachers told me that their zest for learning was amazing, and this, in turn, encouraged the teachers to give their best.

The Science Festival attendees span a wide age range. Within this group are the 'loyalty patrons', comprised mainly of retirees who, despite age, have strongly supported the BSA by regular attendance at the festivals. Being a small group allowed us to get to know each other better: some had been university academicians, whilst most others had been engineers, geologists, teachers, electronics experts and people in various other fields. One was a former barrister turned scientist. Gouri and I were the only medical doctors!

The group is invited to meet the Chief Executive and their team at each Festival. They give us a short account of how the BSA functions, plan innovations, announce dates and venues of future meetings, and seek our views.

The host's students are recruited to help at the festivals, for they know the local layout and are recognisable by a distinctive brightly coloured tee-shirt displaying the venue and year. A senior member of the team very kindly allowed me to purchase shirts at different venues – and I would wear these with pride when at the gym!

Many of the sessions ran in parallel, making it difficult to attend all the talks of interest. In a compact single campus, such as at Hull, there was sufficient time to get from one building to another – but there was no possibility of attending all events. This was partially compensated for by 'The X-Change', which was held at the end of the day's programme in the relaxed atmosphere of the Students Union bar. The event chairperson would invite several of the day's speakers onto the stage to summarise their presentations, followed by a Question & Answer session. Thus, attendees got a flavour of the lectures they could not get to. Many commented that this was a wonderful forum.

Whilst recovering from a major cardiac setback, I tried to build up my stamina by going on walks across open fields near where I lived. During these walks, I would listen to podcasts, and on one occasion, I heard a professor being interviewed about the electronic detection of odours. I met the professor in Manchester, and he gave a fascinating account of his work: I was 'hooked' – and my interest in 'electronic noses' was born, and from this, PhDs and MDs emerged!

Let me mention a few examples to give an idea of the wide variety of subjects presented at these meetings.

At the Brighton meeting in 2017 there was a brilliant presentation by one of the professors who was working on the Cassini space mission to Saturn.

The Science Festival allowed me to meet Sir Harold Kroto, who discovered the C60 version of carbon, called 'Buckminsterfullerene' – more commonly known as 'Buckyball'. He shared the Nobel Prize for Chemistry with Robert Curl and Richard Smalley. He spoke brilliantly and gave a truly gripping account of the nature of discovery.

At Hull, we were introduced to artificial intelligence (AI). It was fascinating as the talk was delivered at the annual dinner to which we were all invited. At the entrance, there were robots serving drinks, and there was a Rubik's cube on each table. You had to test your ability against the robot to solve the Rubik's cube.

At one such event, I was introduced to some aspects of aerospace medicine by a professor who had worked with NASA's Human Adaptation and Countermeasures Office at Johnson Space Centre in Houston.

Areas of social medicine, future medical practice, sleep patterns, and social history since World War II were among my many subjects of interest.

It was at Hull that we met Alex Metcalfe, who gave us a unique insight into trees. He organised a demonstration outside the hall where a tree was festooned with headsets through which people could listen to pre-recorded sounds when listening to live recordings; however, I really got the message. Alex had developed a highly sensitive microphone, shaped like a 'Pinard', the metal device used by midwives to listen to the foetal heart during my medical school days in India. The shape was deliberately chosen as Alex wanted to create a 'visceral' connection, as though listening to a foetal heart. I could now hear 'clicks' caused by 'cavitation', the physical phenomenon created when moving water mixes with air. There was also a lower frequency sound caused by the effect of vibration from the tree moving in the wind.

I recalled learning about xylem and phloem during my schooldays in India and felt a need to brush up! In short, the xylem moves water and minerals from the roots up the plant, flowing only in one direction. Photosynthesis in the leaves produces food substances, which are moved through the phloem, up and down, a more complex process.

While searching Google for further information, I came across a book called 'The Hidden Life of Trees' by Peter Wohlleben. He is an expert in tree ecology. Trees are as complex as human beings, acting as a community for the betterment of all.

For example, when a tree is injured or ill, its compatriots support it by sharing their stores of food. As a result, trees in a natural forest thrive and live long, even beyond a hundred years. Life in the 'slow lane' is complex, and the role of nutrients is self-evident. It turns out that microbes among the root systems have a major influence, similar to our gut microbes.

This reminds me of the forty-year-old silver birch tree in our back garden. We noticed it was shedding large branches for no obvious reason, and it seemed to be swaying excessively. Our wonderful neighbour called in an expert tree surgeon for help. It was thought that the most likely cause was an incurable fungal infection affecting the trunk and roots and that it would need to be cut down.

After our visit to Hull and reading the 'Hidden Life of Trees', I realised that the shedding of large branches was probably a distress call from our tree. It is fascinating and very humbling to know that communication in nature takes such different forms.

A Personal Journey

Incident, insight - - - redemption!

September 1983

A fiery sensation gripped my throat. It lasted a few minutes and gradually faded. The sensation returned on the next two nights, each time after dinner. I was not particularly bothered by it and concluded mild acid reflux was the cause. Gouri was concerned by these developments, particularly when a further episode was more troublesome. I had to go to Gothenburg the next morning to meet with the research team at AstraZeneca to help develop a clinical trial with Omeprazole for acid reflux. My heart was set on this, and nothing was going to stop me!

Earlier I had worked with Cimetidine but now had the opportunity of investigating Omeprazole, the first of a new class of drugs, the proton pump inhibitors (PPI). This was more powerful than Cimetidine, reducing acid secretion by eighty per cent. This raised the possibility of controlling ultra-refractory DU and gastro-oesophageal reflux, a condition that had been steadily increasing.

I set off to Gothenburg feeling optimistic that all would be well. The six-hour meeting was very constructive, as were the discussions over dinner. I deliberately ate only a little, apologising to my hosts for not having more of their delightful Swedish cuisine, my excuse being that I could not gorge myself, discuss and take notes simultaneously!

An old friend from my medical school days came to collect me the next morning and take me to his home, where I would stay that night. It was a beautiful day, so he suggested we stroll in the park. After walking just a short distance, I suddenly felt like all my energy had disappeared. I likened this to a balloon deflating rapidly! The enforced stop allowed me to recover quickly, but on walking again very slowly, I had to stop repeatedly and started to feel sick. My friend, a cardiac surgeon, feared my symptoms were angina, indicative of heart problems. I dismissed his concerns, insisting that my problems were those of acid reflux, a field in which I had a growing interest!

Nevertheless, he 'hijacked' me to his hospital. He pleaded with me to take Aspirin and Metoprolol to protect my heart, just in case it was true angina, and to take Glyceryl trinitrate (GTN) tablets to relieve my symptoms. I countered that GTN also relieves oesophageal (gullet) spasm, which causes very similar symptoms. He wanted me to have an electrocardiogram (ECG) immediately but reluctantly agreed to my compromise that I would have one as soon as I was back at my hospital. On reflection, the delay was unwise, but subconsciously, I must have thought that if there was an abnormality, I might not be able to return home the next morning!

Later, we gently strolled through a new store, IKEA, which had developed a different concept of furniture construction. We stayed there for about two hours, mainly because it was indoors and there was plenty of room to sit down and rest.

My friend dropped me off at the airport early the next morning, reinforcing his advice. Later I learnt that he had phoned Gouri to tell her of his concerns!

During the flight, I had two or three episodes of 'fire in the throat' but with a difference; this was the first time it had occurred in the daytime, and relief came only after I had the 'inner urge' to grip my seat armrests and arch my back. Seeing my 'manoeuvres', the gentleman in the aisle seat, who earlier had extolled the aerial views of Sweden, quietly moved to the back of the half-empty aircraft!

That night I awoke with a peculiar, hard-to-describe 'awareness' of my upper teeth, which compelled me to wash my mouth! The sensation passed, and I resumed my sleep.

The next morning I started my outpatient clinic at the Montagu Hospital. The first patient had chest symptoms, so I sent him for an ECG just four rooms down the corridor. The second patient did not show up, so I crept into the ECG room and cheekily asked my patient if I could have the test first, as I had to return to the clinic shortly! The technician was hesitant but finally gave in! The nursing staff found out and in alarm, rushed in; I assured them that all was well and would be even better if I could have a mug of tea! I put the ECG tracing in my briefcase without examining it closely, confident or hoping it would be normal.

I saw several other patients in the course of that long morning. At the end of the clinic, I rushed over to Rotherham Hospital to start my long gastroscopy list that afternoon. Whilst carrying out the procedures, my excellent registrar, who was training with me, enquired about some papers we needed to discuss. I pointed to my briefcase and began the next examination. The registrar found the ECG in my briefcase and asked whose it was as it was abnormal. I replied that it was mine, countering that such mild changes could be recognised in gallstone colic and that early reports suggested it may also occur in acid reflux. The poor chap was disturbed, but he did not pursue the matter since I was feeling fine and getting on with the list. However, he phoned home that evening to let Gouri know of his concerns and to ask how I was.

Things changed abruptly that night! The fiery sensation in my throat recurred, spread down, and was troublesome. I instinctively knelt, gripped a chair and braced myself. The attack eased. The next one did not, so I took GTN, which relieved the symptoms rapidly, a coincidence as the effect was almost immediate. I slept but awoke shortly after that with more severe symptoms. Alarmed, Gouri phoned our GP and close friend who lived nearby. He called for an ambulance, then rushed over, and having little doubt about the true nature of the problem, he gave me an injection of morphine. The ambulance people, who knew me, were astonished, but I could not remember much.

I awoke in our Coronary Care Unit (CCU). The patient in the next bed was perhaps 'impressed' by my 'dedication' for he was under my care and due to be reviewed later that morning! The next day the poor chap suffered a cardiac arrest. Instinctively I reacted. Although restricted by ECG monitoring leads and an intravenous drip, I jumped out of bed and managed to defibrillate him successfully after the third shock! I thought I had done reasonably well, but Matron, an energetic lady hardened during the war years, rushed over and 'scolded' me, but only out of genuine concern that "something" might have happened to me during my "antics". I tried logic, saying that the resuscitation team would have taken two or three minutes to arrive, whereas I had the job done in seconds. It is a fact that in cardiac arrest, seconds count! She was not impressed, nor were the nurses. I realised I was not going to convince Matron or the nurses, so I kept quiet!

Matron was concerned that I might try to "escape" to my office downstairs to get on with some work. So she instructed the nursing staff to hide my clothes. I later learnt that she thought I would not dare to walk out wearing only a hospital gown, which would expose my backside!

So how did I, a consultant now for ten years, get things so wrong? I was "only forty-three", fit, a non-smoker and a regular squash player. A couple of months earlier, the National Coal Board's Medical Director showed his new 'state of the art' exercise-ECG treadmill to an invited group of consultants. I volunteered to take the test. The Director congratulated me on my fitness, adding that I was good enough to be considered for coal mine rescue duties!

I thanked him but commented that I was rather small. He replied that it would be fine as I could be lowered into places the big lads could not reach!

A deeper reason for my diagnostic error, as I learnt with time, was rooted in one of my many character flaws: interests become obsessions, which I pursue impervious to advice from others. Such pursuit, however, has some advantages; it led my team and me to develop new research programmes, which in turn helped patients and guided the careers of several young doctors in my team.

I had hoped to initiate the first patients in the new Omeprazole trial on 1 December 1983. I did this, but only from a distance, lying in bed at home recovering from cardiac surgery! My Registrar enrolled the first patient, and soon many more followed. After a short period of enforced rest, I returned to work. The clinical trial results transformed the management of refractory peptic ulcers, leading to a substantial reduction in surgery. Omeprazole was also effective in controlling the rising tide of acid reflux.

Symptoms such as my own came to be called 'unstable' or 'crescendo' angina, the outcome being high mortality! My experience opened a new avenue of investigation, revealing that distinguishing acid reflux from angina was often more difficult than it first appeared because the two conditions frequently co-exist. Indeed, a few years later, a young doctor from Manchester whom I had met a few times at a regional meeting demonstrated that acid refluxing back into the gullet diminishes blood flow through the coronary arteries!

Some of my patients with peptic ulcer disease or acid reflux died unexpectedly over the years from heart attacks. This alerted our group to such diagnostic confusion and reshaped our clinical practice many years before this became commonplace. As a result, we were able to help numerous patients, and I will illustrate this with two examples.

A colleague called in at my outpatient clinic at Rotherham Hospital about another matter. He mentioned in passing that he was burping a lot, particularly when going upstairs. Now aware of the possibility of diagnostic confusion, I walked up the staircase with him, confirmed his symptoms and arranged for an exercise ECG. The consultant cardiologist, a family friend, chided me for not referring our colleague to him for formal exercise ECG. I accepted this but pointed out that the waiting list for the procedure was at least a couple of weeks, whereas my unconventional approach gave the diagnosis immediately. Following a coronary bypass operation the next week, our colleague was soon on the mend, as I saw for myself when I visited him at home!

The second example is that of a GP who telephoned me in the clinic complaining that his ulcer was back. I had successfully treated his duodenal ulcer several years before, but as his story unfolded, I sensed there were now subtle differences. Reluctantly he agreed to have an exercise ECG after finishing his clinic. As you may have guessed, the test was positive, and he soon recovered after coronary bypass surgery!

The Day-3 Blues

I have had multiple problems over the years caused by coronary artery disease, which reduces blood flow to the heart's muscles. The effect ranges from chest pain, which can be disabling, to the actual 'death' of part of the heart muscles, technically termed myocardial infarction, and better known as 'heart attack'. I have been rescued at various times by different levels of intervention, from which I learnt a lot.

In addition, each setback opened new possibilities, some of which my team and I were able to develop into fresh lines of research. Most would regard this as 'unusual' for my main area of work is in gastroenterology, which is concerned with disorders of the digestive tract. Little wonder that friends and colleagues regard me as a benign eccentric!

A heart attack is caused by a clot blocking a coronary artery, so the patient's veins are used to create a route for blood to bypass the blockage. Such operations are now common, but matters were different three to four decades ago. These historical reflections will hopefully give the reader an insight into the past. My first coronary artery bypass graft (CABG) was on the fifth of November in 1983.

I had experienced what I thought was 'heartburn' for about a week, regarding it as acid reflux, not least because my symptoms resembled those of many patients I had treated for this condition. In addition, I was only forty-three and a fit squash player.

I was discharged from the Coronary Care Unit to rest at home for a short period before returning to work, particularly as I was otherwise physically fit and restless being housebound.

My cardiologist and the cardiac surgeon made a decision for me to have a coronary angiogram. The cardiologist expected the findings to be normal or, at most, to show only minimal changes. Gouri and I were puzzled when he came to see us after the procedure and was hesitant, which was very unlike him. He told us that I needed to have a CABG, which had a low mortality of one to two per cent. A healthy spectator would regard such odds as excellent, but when the gun is pointed at your head, matters look very different. After all, I might draw the short straw and be that one person in a hundred who would die during the operation.

A couple of days later, the cardiac surgeon kindly phoned to check my progress. To my surprise, I found it impossible to walk unassisted from the bedroom to the bathroom, only a few steps away. He said he wanted me to come to the surgical ward at two o'clock that afternoon (a Friday) and that he would operate on Sunday morning. He jokingly added that he thought I was an idiot as a registrar but seemed no better as a consultant. He could not understand how I could have possibly mistaken my symptoms for anything other than severe angina.

At the time, Gouri worked as a locum consultant haematologist at Doncaster Royal Infirmary. I phoned her with the news, which she took in quietly. I could only imagine her dilemma as there was a real chance of being widowed with two young children. Her colleagues comforted her, adding that the cardiothoracic surgeon was very good and that all would be well.

I was assured that I would be home on the seventh day. Three days post-operatively, my personality began to change. For much of my life, I was in trouble for being boisterous or cracking jokes at the wrong time, but Gouri told me I seemed to have withdrawn into a deep and dark cave and even turned my back on my family.

The surgeon commented that I had the day-three blues, a term I had never heard of. He assured me, however, that I would get over this by the end of the week. The next few days were difficult. I refused to use the commode at the bedside; instead, I clutched a small pillow to my chest and walked to the toilet. The nurses were terrified as there was a risk of my collapse. A wonderful thing then happened: a junior nurse sang to me to lift my spirits. Previously a junior nurse in my ward at Rotherham, the staff nurse was taking a patient to the Radiology Department for a chest X-ray. She also took me along "to see the big world outside". I felt much better. These are wonderful examples of common sense, kindness and human touches that rescued me from despair.

I was to be discharged on Sunday, but by Saturday, I became really desperate to leave. I had completely broken down and pleaded with the consultant to be allowed to leave, repeatedly saying I had made my peace with my God and just wanted to be at home. He reluctantly agreed, and an hour later, I was back home, greeted by my wife, family, and our delightful GP. I just wanted to get upstairs to the bedroom, but my GP insisted I stop and rest at each step. My breathlessness made this inevitable. My concern was that I had developed heart failure, but later I learned that cardiac surgeons deliberately do not correct anaemia; as a result, the circulation speeds up, reducing the chances of blockages in the grafts.

It was wonderful being home. Very thoughtfully, Gouri had placed a small TV set near the foot of the bed. Curiously, even after all these years, I recall the name of the programme 'For Britain and for the Hell of It', which described Donald Campbell's speedboat racing records.

A week later, I started to walk along Moorgate Road, with Gouri following in the car! By week two, a dear family friend began to accompany me on walks and helped me to build up pace steadily. I still recall some oddities on walks, for example, dog poo on the pathways, into which I occasionally stepped! When cold, I wore a balaclava, and when I stepped into our local post office, I was puzzled why the staff appeared uncomfortable, despite knowing me for years. It seemed a similarly dressed man had threatened staff at some Rotherham post offices. There was much relief once I removed the balaclava!

Gouri was due to be interviewed for a consultant post at Doncaster Royal Infirmary. She phoned to say she had been appointed. I shouted with joy and never looked back from that time onwards. My mother, who was staying with us, was apprehensive about my celebrating Sonny's birthday at the Whiston parish hall nearby. It must have been a strange sight as I wore my thick duffle coat, but Sonny and his friends enjoyed the evening, and that was all that mattered to me.

A few days later I began to run, and to continue running as it was a joy to no longer feel imprisoned within myself.

A GP whom I knew slightly would keep me company during my runs along the main roads near our house. He told me about the power of meditation and that one could do this whilst running. At the time, I had no interest in meditation and did not want to consider it during runs as I thought it would be a distraction on busy roads.

Many of my patients visited me at home; such was their kindness and generosity. Once back at work, some of my patients with digestive disorders who also needed a coronary bypass wanted to have a longer consultation, *not* about their tummy but to gain insight into the operation based on my experience!

My cardiac surgeon phoned me some months after my operation requesting that I see a GP who had had CABG recently and was badly affected by the day-three blues, its symptoms lingering. The GP explained he felt sure something had gone wrong in Intensive Care, perhaps to do with the equipment, a belief he was unable to shake off. Thank goodness I had the sense not to argue but to simply recount my experience returning to full-time work and enjoying it. Regrettably, I did not get the opportunity to follow up as I was back to my long working hours.

Let me add this explanatory note about the day-three blues and coronary artery bypass. The blood from the body has to go through an oxygenator, which puts oxygen into the blood. It was later realised that actual bubbles of oxygen get into the blood and can cause bizarre changes in the brain and, at least in part, maybe the explanation for those blues.

I learnt an important lesson from my own day-three blues, which has guided me ever since: I would never ever tell a patient with similar problems to "pull yourself together".

Soon I was back to normal, even to the extent of disregarding advice and taking up squash! It was great fun.

Unusual symptoms

When walking in the cold, I could feel tightening, indeed pain, in the face, jaws and chest, which was very difficult to explain. My colleague tested me in the consultants' car park on a particularly cold day. With ECG leads fitted, I walked around with my top covered only by my shirt until symptoms developed, and I could go no further, yet the ECG was normal.

I finally decided to ensure I was well wrapped up when out on walks, in response to which my friends commented that I had at last shown some evidence of common sense!

I was very pleased to be fit again, go to the gym, and work long hours with my marvellous team, which led to other advances.

Cardiac Arrest: Return of the foe!

The once familiar symptoms returned, striking with little or no warning, particularly when outside and worse when cold: jaw ache, breathlessness even after seemingly little effort, and central chest pain. These steadily worsened.

My GP referred me to my physician and the Consultant Cardiologist at the Northern General Hospital. Coronary angiography in May 1996 showed narrowing of the arteries in several places, such that a further bypass operation would not help, nor would inserting a stent to create an alternative channel for blood to flow through as such technology had not been developed.

I was advised to make the best of what little time I had left.

Being beyond medical help left me 'free' to do what I liked most: continue as before! I could still go to the gym but eventually had to give up playing squash – a pity!

Coping

Let me give you examples of coping with daily life when the heart is badly deprived of its blood flow: I will concentrate on practicalities aided by medical knowledge and 'bloody-minded stubbornness'!

The following is an example of a typical week.

I reduced major angina attacks by triggering gentler episodes!

On endoscopy mornings, I would be on my feet for most of the time, so I would run up the steps from the car park and dash to my office whilst carrying several rucksacks.

I learned from my cardiac surgeon that he and his colleagues were familiar with this technically termed "ischaemic pre-conditioning" strategy.

Think of it as a form of 'vaccination'. Flu injections may cause mild symptoms but prevent a major debilitating attack. By chance, I became aware that reducing sleep midweek helped me to stay alert at work! The same was true for changing eating habits: snacking through the day and having a proper meal only in the evening, even if reduced.

Troublesome mouth ulcers – my indicator of increasing stress – developed invariably by Friday and made eating painful. A tablet of Temazepam on Friday or Saturday, followed by a deep long sleep, helped greatly and not uncommonly, I could start the next week with my mouth free of ulcers. Through "trial and error", I learnt that the timing of Temazepam was important: taken too early, I would fall asleep before I could eat – but when taken after food, it would not have any effect!

Cardiac arrest

Let me return to the fateful day in July 2002. On Saturday, 21 July, I carried out a long all-day gastroscopy list and examined 54 patients to support the hospital Chairman's charity appeal. Tiring but exhilarating!

The next day I was working in my office, and to shake off any residual tiredness, I decided to run up the stairs to the top floor of the hospital. Level 'D' to 'C' was OK, but chest and jaw pain developed from 'C' to 'B'. From 'B' to 'A' the pain rapidly worsened – and the last thing I recalled was being a few steps from the top. A short distance from the Coronary Care Unit entrance, a visitor noticed me collapsed on the landing. With commendable resourcefulness, he dashed back to the Unit and asked the nursing staff for help, and they immediately called '222': the 'crash call'.

Embarrassingly, my team and I were on duty that day! The youngsters were horrified to see the "Boss" collapsed, but our registrar rallied them around, and they immediately started external cardiac massage. I was surprised to learn that I had been 'writhing' for some time before defibrillation brought me back to life. In recovery, I asked my cardiologist to explain how I could be dead and writhing! He commented that it happens but was at a loss to explain the mechanism.

The cardiologist arranged my urgent transfer to the Northern General Hospital (NGH) that afternoon. The effects of intravenous painkillers wore off at night. The NGH cardiologist had a chat with me the next morning. I said I was dead for a few moments but was fine now, so I should be allowed to go home to get on with my work. He muttered something about obstinacy and, understandably, refused!

Instead, he said he would attempt stenting as the technology had advanced considerably since May 1996. I was placed on the angiogram table and given sedation. Amazingly it had not the slightest effect, so very different from the many thousands of patients in whom my team and I used the drug routinely! As I was awake, I asked the consultant whether I could watch him perform the procedure. He obliged and gave me a running commentary - a wonderful 'master class'. I returned home a couple of days later feeling much better.

Back to my duties at Rotherham Hospital

I was deeply moved by the enormous concern and goodwill of many staff members and patients.

I was instructed to work only part-time, but, knowing my restless nature, our management staff changed the pattern of my work instead. Strangely, far from being a constraint, it opened up many new avenues, several of which led to major developments!

I had a further setback on Boxing Day 2008. I am ever grateful to the very brave cardiothoracic surgeon who undertook my second cardiac bypass after warning me that the operation had risks similar to "a champagne flute being dissected out of a block of concrete". The second bypass was a success, and this little poem brings together my feelings about the event.

The son et Lumiere of the cardiac surgery intensive care unit

Dimmed lights, darkness

Quiet yet with musical interruption

Glowing screens, sinuous waves gliding across

Symmetrical asymmetry of my ECG punctuated by wandering P waves

Numbers: can this really be me?

The triple rising peep-peep-peep of infusion pumps demanding attention

The five-note staccato reply of other machinery, R2D2-like (in Star Wars)

The bong-bong-bong of my intra-aortic balloon pump

Replied by my neighbour's, when we both moved legs

The gentle whoosh-whir of warm air filling the special heat blankets

The confusion of darkness, the morphine-mirages

Who are all these people? Why are they trying to sell me insurance?

The kindly re-assurance of my nurse that there really were no strangers

The gentle yet firm practised nursing hands turning taps on my many lines

Drawing blood silently, the results are instantly available,

My cardboard tongue relieved by a delightful taste of buttered toast at 5 a.m.

Of life-enhancing winter sunlight at last breaking through to start the new day

I am now declining both physically and mentally. As a result, Gouri and I have made advanced directives against resuscitation with our excellent GP.

From hallucination - - - to terror!

I was in my study late on the night of 16 January 2017; deeply immersed in preparing a special lecture I was to deliver in Kolkata in February when I 'sensed a presence'. Whipping around, I saw our family friend and computer genius. He had his index finger to his lips and whispered that we should not wake up Gouri. He wanted to know how the presentation was coming on. And with that, he vanished as mysteriously as he had appeared.

I was *not* studying but in bed, trying to get over the 'flu'. I dashed to the front bedroom where Gouri was recovering from intestinal obstruction and told her what had happened. She assured me that no one else was around, so I crept back to bed. Shortly afterwards, I jumped out again, put on the lights, checked the house alarm, dashed downstairs, and inspected every door, front, back and garage. All secure. Still unconvinced, I went through the garage onto the driveway. I saw nothing amiss and was beaten back by the cold and dark.

I returned to bed but some time later jumped out again and repeated the performance with the same results. As morning broke, I drove to the hospital to work with my two colleagues and friends. It was rapidly becoming clear that it was unsafe for me to fly out to Kolkata. Consequently, we decided to adapt to new technology, overlaying each PowerPoint slide with its unique soundtrack. My son urged me to concentrate on the storyline and select PowerPoint slides to illustrate the theme and assured me he would take care of the soundtrack technology.

The restlessness continued through the next two or three nights, along with a troublesome hacking cough, running nose, and generally feeling miserable. Of greater concern to Gouri was my behaviour, which had become even more erratic and irrational!

Gouri got in touch with our friend and colleague, the Consultant Microbiologist. Preliminary blood tests revealed abnormalities which required further exploration. He kindly arranged for the phlebotomy team to see me in his office to take various blood samples whilst his microbiology team took urine and sputum. Once in his office, however, I was gripped by foreboding, a real fear that people were 'out to get me and hurt me'.

It is in my nature to look at things differently. I reasoned that my 'tormentors' would ambush me at the corner, and accordingly, I planned a different move; two and a half steps in a circle. I was sent to the Radiology Department, where the CT scan showed no evidence of a stroke, which had been a real concern, but the chest X-ray revealed an infection. ECG showed no new changes. I was then taken to the Chest Physician. To my surprise, I was unable to string even a few words together, so Gouri had to tell him of my symptoms. He prescribed Doxycycline; this was troubling as I have seen patients where this drug has damaged the gullet. Nevertheless, I collected the drug, and with the treatment, I slowly started to improve.

The final diagnosis was post-infection psychosis in the elderly.

Recovering my former mental state took several months. Fortunately, I was able to build up strength and weight in the gym. As ever, my mind would not rest, so I adapted some of the furniture at home for power and stability exercises, useful when I could not go to the gym.

My illness mystified me as I had the flu vaccine shortly before going to the USA. I learnt from the microbiologist that the vaccine protects seventy-five per cent of those who stay in the UK. If an infection is acquired overseas, however, protection is far less. Indeed, my first sign of illness developed on the overnight flight back to Manchester when unexpectedly I was struck by diarrhoea. The blood, urine and sputum tests confirmed I had an ongoing coinfection with various organisms, and so the choice of Doxycycline was excellent.

Postscript

I reflected on my experience and recalled incidents of 'confusion in the elderly' in two of my patients.

The first occurred during my ward rounds. Just as I approached the next bay, an elderly lady screamed, "Get him out of here, get him out of here!" I was puzzled, but she insisted there was an "evil clown" who had hurt her!

Her changed behaviour was because I had started her on steroids to dampen inflammation of her arteries, which, if unchecked, might cause blindness. Necessity forced me to use a high dose, one side effect being hallucinations. The lady improved rapidly once I reduced the dose, and she remained well.

The second patient was a Welsh ex-miner whom I had looked after for many years and managed to get rid of his once-troublesome duodenal ulcer. He and his wife were truly lovely and gentle, and they came to see me at home after my first coronary bypass in 1983 out of concern and friendship.

Many years later, he was admitted to the ward feeling generally unwell. The next evening he tried to jump out of the window! Being small and wiry, he could have managed it but was stopped by the nurses in the nick of time.

He was upset and felt "guilty". I assured him there was no reason to feel upset or guilty as he had a urinary tract infection which had not caused the usual symptoms such as frequency and burning when passing water. Instead, it had caused his behaviour to change, technically termed psychosis. He recovered fully after antibiotic treatment. I was so relieved to have been able to help them.

I have repeatedly told my medical students and junior doctors that I have learnt much from medical school teachers and my seniors as a consultant. But it is from the patients I have had the privilege to serve that I have learnt the most, and I am eternally grateful to them.

Memories from Trips Abroad

A plague of pimples

January 1993

Professor Israel Nathan 'Solly' Marks, Professor of Gastroenterology at the famous Groote Schuur Hospital, had invited me to give a series of lectures at various major centres in South Africa. It was a busy and exhilarating experience during which I developed a peculiar medical problem.

After lectures in Pretoria and Johannesburg, my hosts kindly arranged for me to have a short break at a game park before returning to Cape Town to give further lectures and teach medical students. To protect myself against spiders and insects, I wore full-sleeved shirts, sports socks, trainers and a hat, thus minimising bare skin. I was warned not to leave the camp for a stroll as wild animals lurked nearby!

The day after returning to Cape Town, I awoke early, puzzled by the numerous pimples I was covered with, some of them very large. I was alarmed as there was blood on my clothes and the bathroom floor! I had never come across such a problem; logic should have guided my thinking, but my mind froze!

As arranged, I went to Prof Marks's department late that morning before joining medical students in the afternoon for a teaching session. Whilst with Solly, I mentioned my strange affliction. He was also baffled, so he took me to the Professor of Dermatology. She was also uncertain, so she arranged for a skin biopsy that afternoon.

The Professor requested her registrar, a middle-grade trainee, to do the biopsy. He had very recently arrived from Harare, the capital of Zimbabwe. He recognised the problem instantly and, to my relief, advised that a biopsy was not necessary. He dramatically plucked one of the large pimples and placed it next to me on the couch. To my utter amazement, the pimple 'walked away'! Not to be outdone, I plucked off a few more of varying sizes. The registrar squashed one, and out came blood! Answer? Ticks! Familiarity and experience really do increase one's confidence. These creatures attach themselves to the victim's skin and resemble a freckle. They gorge on blood overnight, often drop off and walk away, presumably to have a good snooze after their drinking session! I thought I had been fully protected, so I did not expect a successful sneak attack by these crafty creatures.

Having made the diagnosis, the question arose: how does one treat it? Uncertainty is common in medicine, and the prevailing view was that half of the patients get better spontaneously, whereas the other half benefits from tetracycline. I was advised against treatment, which would protect me from drug-induced side effects, and to hope for the best!

The rest of my stay in Cape Town was fine. At the final stop in Durban, I started to feel unwell. To recover in preparation for a major lecture I had to give that night, I went for a swim. I had underestimated the power of the waves and was thrown about, grazing myself repeatedly on the underlying sand, the equivalent of being scrubbed by sandpaper!

The next day I met various people at the teaching hospital, enjoyed very engaging discussions, and, later that evening, set off on my return journey to the UK. As a precaution, I phoned my wonderful registrar and asked him to check on treatment alternatives.

By the time I got back to Rotherham, I was itching badly. I took a full course of Tetracycline and felt better, but the itching was a real problem. I went to see the Professor of Infectious Diseases at the Hallamshire Hospital. He was fascinated by my predicament and took endless photographs, which he wanted to show at a national dermatology meeting. He brought the consultation to an end, and he was puzzled when I looked a little crestfallen as I was hoping he would advise on treatment. There was little one could do other than apply the cream. The itching was to trouble me for many months before eventually subsiding.

An important lesson

Always check whether there has been any recent overseas travel preceding the development of an unfamiliar skin condition.

An arresting moment

It was a beautiful morning in Cape Town. I was struck by the grandeur of the building's gleaming white high walls decorated with a beautiful logo. Just as I snapped the third picture, I heard an angry voice shouting behind me, making me turn: there stood a furious young white officer accompanied by two large black uniformed police. I was arrested and, with my host, Professor Solly Marks, and a colleague, ordered to follow them through the gates nearby to the commandant's office. This was the Pollsmoor Prison to which the legendary Nelson Mandela was to be transferred after his incarceration on Robben Island, a short distance offshore.

At least I was spared the handcuffs. Once inside the compound and joined by yet more policemen, I could see the prisoners' wing high above, where several black inmates shouted, "Take a picture of me, bass", and so forth. Solly ordered me to put away my camera as we were already in enough trouble.

I was apprehensive when we entered the commandant's office, a room of modest size which, when filled with the large number of officials, mainly uniformed police, was very cramped, intimidating in fact.

The commandant questioned me for a while, and it gradually became apparent that this 'foreigner' from Britain was not a troublemaking journalist. This was a genuine mistake made by a medical doctor who had been invited to lecture in his area of research. He informed me that it was illegal to photograph any government building or anybody in uniform. I commented that this was a serious omission from my Berlitz pocket guide! He softened, so I asked if I could not take a picture of the building, could I take a picture of Robben Island hanging on the wall behind him. He saw the funny side but told me not to push my luck!

How very embarrassing and how very different from the way the day started!

It was an eventful lecture tour as I saw four major centres, including the famous Groote Schuur Hospital in Cape Town. I was able to give talks on research areas we shared, principally peptic ulcers. In addition, I was invited to join ward rounds, exchange views with South African physicians and surgeons, and so on. Indeed, I was made most welcome throughout my stay in South Africa.

I joined the gastroenterology team on ward rounds in the morning. Such rounds are traditionally led by consultants with long years of experience, but many had emigrated. So the youngsters, who in Britain would be regarded as middle-grade trainees, were now taking on a major role; this included making difficult decisions. It is always impressive and inspiring to see youngsters stepping up to a senior role, which reminded me of my early days!

The patients we encountered had a wide range of disorders. I was familiar with the majority, but interestingly, gut diseases like ulcerative colitis and Crohn's disease behave differently in Cape Town, where the population affected is diverse. Some patients had conditions I knew almost nothing about. There was a lot to discuss, and I was most grateful for this unique opportunity.

After the rounds, we sat down for refreshments in the ward sister's office. She apologised for not offering lavish refreshments. She provided us with various fruits and juices, which I was very pleased to have, and we had a wonderful day.

My big lecture was on the following night. There was a huge audience. Prof Marks went to the podium to introduce me. "Today, our guest speaker is a recently released prisoner. No, not Nelson Mandela but Chandu Bardhan from Rotherham in the UK." There was a lot of laughter! The lecture went well and provoked many discussions. I was relieved and encouraged.

The evening before I left for the UK, the Gastroenterology Department gathered to bid me farewell. Prof Marks spoke first and then invited my comments. I said I was deeply inspired by my visit. I truly admired the spirit of enterprise in the difficult circumstances the staff faced. I added that at Rotherham and all over the UK, I sensed that we had lost something precious, namely, the spirit which I had seen in South Africa. For my colleagues and me, the problem was increasing bureaucratic control.

Over the next several years, I met the consultants and youngsters at various meetings, sometimes in the USA and Europe and on one occasion in London.

And there the matter ended, I thought. But twelve years later, in 2005, Prof Marks phoned to ask what I was currently doing. I told him my role had changed. Solly said he had been summoned out of retirement to help run the unit and asked whether I might visit again to take over from him. I compromised by offering to visit on six weeks sabbatical to 'test the water', not least because my wife Gouri was concerned that my health would no longer permit me to act as I would have in my younger days! The Dean of the Medical School added his invitation as well.

Times certainly had changed in South Africa. The new Dean of the medical school in Cape Town was a native African. He was also the Vice Chancellor; one of his protégés, also a native African, had taken over the Dean's previous position. Sadly, Prof Marks passed away. I was honoured to be asked to contribute a eulogy to the South African medical journal.

Kazakhstan

I received an email out of the blue from Dr Cherian Thomas (Titu), my dear friend from medical school at Vellore, asking me to join him on a trip to Kazakhstan, specifically to Semipalatinsk (Semey). Titu was a Professor of Medicine in India for almost twenty-three years. He then served on the Board of the Global Health Ministries of the United Methodist Church in New York City. Titu covered the international section.

Titu had worked in difficult regions like Liberia, Sierra Leone, the Congo and Mozambique, all of which had their share of civil conflicts. He had worked with a range of medical missionaries, including Dr Christiana Hena, a family practitioner who was our guide during our stay in Kazakhstan.

I had heard of Kazakhstan and was dimly aware that it was somewhere close to Russia; that was the sum total of my knowledge! The plan was that Titu would fly out from New York and me from Manchester, and we would meet in Amsterdam. From there, we would fly to Almaty, the largest city in Kazakhstan. Checking on the map, I noticed it was almost at the same longitude as New Delhi: in other words, it would be a long flight!

We were greeted at Almaty by a Russian lady who had come down overnight by train to receive us. Titu and I spent one night at a hotel in Almaty and then flew out in a turboprop aeroplane on the short flight to Semey. The engine cowlings were flapping, which struck me as odd. I took comfort, however, from the fact that the plane had made repeated trips without mishap! Another 'unusual' feature was the seatbelts or the lack of them! As we entered the plane, we could see our luggage heaped up and restrained only by wire netting, and not everyone had a seatbelt! Nevertheless, we arrived in high spirits.

Dr Hena met us at the airport and drove us to the Irtysh Hotel, named after the river. We were later introduced to our host, the Professor of Surgery

Semey was downwind from the Russian nuclear testing grounds and only sixty-five miles east of The Polygon test site, where a monument had been built to honour those who had died from radiation exposure. The professor's research was innovative and far-seeing. He regularly visited Hiroshima, the first city on which the atomic bomb was dropped. Many of those not killed immediately or shortly afterwards went on to develop illnesses, which served as a warning to the Professor of what might happen in Semey.

We stayed at a Soviet Union-styled hotel; the rooms were modest but comfortable, and there were female attendants, all dressed similarly, seated on each floor to help the guests.

We had the opportunity to visit a small hospital in a village called Karaul in northern Kazakhstan, which served the local and surrounding population. Peptic ulcer disease was still common. The hospital was equipped with one of the 'see-through' gastroscopes (as opposed to the modern videoscopes), but it was in good working order. The catch, however, was that the bulb in the Pentax light source had fused, and despite having ordered a replacement over two months before, none had appeared. This was blamed on the usual bureaucratic delays, a leftover from the Soviet days. So, neither their own staff nor I could gastroscope any of the patients we had seen with upper abdominal pain.

In Semey, various types of endoscopes were used in different hospitals. For example, the Department of Surgery in the Emergency Hospital used an old see-through fibrescope of Russian manufacture, which worked despite a fair number of broken fibres; this was something I was familiar with in our older instruments. The endoscopist at Semey nevertheless completed the examination with great skill, the mark of a real expert. In contrast, the Diagnostic Centre, less than one kilometre away, had state-of-the-art Pentax video endoscopes! The disparity reflected the different streams of funding available, and again it showed the rigidity of bureaucratic systems.

The Professor showed me around the medical school, which was located a kilometre or so from the hospital. All the buildings had a name except for one. He saw my puzzled look and explained, "Chandu, here, the West and the Japanese can carry out genetic experiments, which would be forbidden in their home centres!"

The medical school attracted students from various places, including Pakistan. Several of them were familiar with English. In contrast, people from other areas of Kazakhstan and central European countries were less acquainted with the language. The Professor introduced a scheme whereby the teaching faculty would be trained to deliver tuition in English; this proved a success.

We went to visit some patients at their homes. One, in particular, appreciated our efforts and, as a mark of gratitude, flicked his forefinger against his windpipe, which mystified me. The gesture, it turned out, was a cause for celebration, marked by sharing glasses of vodka!

I presumed that many of the attendees would be Kazak Muslims, so I was surprised to learn that several were Christians. It was a wonderful chance to engage with youngsters from different backgrounds.

At the hospital, I saw that breezeblocks were missing from the walls. They had been used for people's homes, not dissimilar to tiles being appropriated for a similar purpose in India! I stopped to take a few photographs of the surroundings when quite suddenly, a couple of sweet nurses grabbed me by my elbows and wanted us to be photographed by one of their fellow nurses; a touching gesture!

Departure

The drive to the airport gave me a chance to see majestic views of the flat steppes and the several isolated huts used by farmers.

The Airport

During check-in for the return flight, I was taken to one side by a senior official who asked me to carry a small suitcase for a British passenger whose luggage had exceeded the allowance, whereas I had relatively little. On reflection, 2004 seems like innocent times; such a 'luggage arrangement' would be strictly forbidden today!

It was wonderful to be back home. The very fact that memories linger so powerfully almost seventeen years later testifies to the impression made.

The BRET Story

I moved from Sheffield to Rotherham with £23, the remnant of a small gift received to support earlier work in Sheffield. Equipment and other necessities were obtained by much scavenging, goodwill and sheer good fortune.

So equipped and spurred on by a long-standing fascination with peptic ulcer disease, I began my research in earnest. In the mid-1970s, histamine H2 receptor antagonists (H2RA) emerged. These were the first drugs that could effectively suppress stomach acid secretion, so they had the potential to heal a peptic ulcer. The research team at Smith Kline & French (SK&F) who pioneered this development became aware of the increasingly strong research interest at Rotherham, and a link was formed. The very first clinical trial proved that Cimetidine, the test drug, was extraordinarily effective in rapidly relieving symptoms and healing the ulcer. The follow-up studies then demonstrated that recurrence could be greatly reduced with a small nightly dose. Rotherham's industries at that time were principally coal and steel, involving heavy work and a fit workforce, but ulcer disease often prevented the victim from working. This medical advance led to fewer deaths from ulcer complications, a rapidly diminishing need for surgery and a speedy return to work.

These studies brought in small amounts of funds from SK&F. As was then the practice, such funds were made to the investigator as a personal payment to be used as he or she saw fit. Gouri, however, urged me to use them for the wider benefit of patients. This led to strengthening clinical gastroenterology, establishing a patient database, ensuring systematic follow-up of all patients and developing the facility for patients to self-refer if problems arose. Importantly, the funds were also used to recruit staff. The remainder was sufficient to start investigating the regulation of acid secretion during the day and night. Such studies on the circadian rhythm led to the first PhD.

From these beginnings, there emerged a model of clinical practice and research, 'from bedside to bench and back to the bedside', a 'virtuous cycle' linking fundamental science, translational medicine and clinical research. A strength of the system was that one could join the cycle at any point.

We were getting better at controlling peptic ulcers, but then another acid-related condition became more noticeable, namely, acid reflux disease. A high dose of Cimetidine was effective in relieving symptoms in several, but it required even stronger therapy for effective control. This led to early studies with proton pump inhibitors (PPI), which proved very effective. As is the nature of research, each advance leads to other opportunities requiring different skills. Thus, issues identified at Rotherham were investigated through 'fundamental science' resulting from collaborations with various university departments in Sheffield, and this led to further PhDs. These collaborations were essentially informal as and when opportunities arose. The increasing volume of joint research, however, required a more formal structure with close monitoring.

The creation of BRET (www.thebret.org)

All funds earned as a result of our collaboration with the pharmaceutical industry, as well as donations from patients and their families, were held in trust by Rotherham Hospital within the Gastroenterology Research Fund (GERF). New rules introduced in the 1980s made this difficult, so a decision was taken to place the funds in a charity created to support our work. The financial director and a lawyer took the plan to the Charity Commission. The creation of the charity was inspired by Gouri as it reflected her deep-held conviction that if a person or family is blessed with good fortune, then it is their moral obligation to share this with others so that together we can all advance. And so The Bardhan Research and Education Trust of Rotherham Limited, which became known as BRET, was formed, incorporated as a company limited by guarantee on 13 April 1988, and entered on the Register of Charities on 21 December 1989. BRET now began to support a wider range of research both at Rotherham and the University of Sheffield, later expanding to other centres, covering PhDs, MDs and post-doctoral Fellowships. At the height of collaboration with pharmaceutical companies, the charity also funded ten members of staff, including research nurses and administrative support.

BRET Board

In the early 1990s, BRET's viability came under question due to the activities of the Financial Director but with the formation of a new, stronger and committed Board, the recovery began. The very nature of BRET allowed Trustees to stay closely in touch with the Research Fellows. From discussions, they recognised the need for 'blue skies' thinking and to risk supporting such projects (where other funding sources were reluctant). Some projects failed, but not for want of trying. Most succeeded, judged not only by the breakthroughs made but also by the personal development of the researchers, many of whom, in later years, went on to great prominence. To date, fifty-four grants totalling in excess of two million pounds sterling have been awarded. Many of these grants were to doctors and scientists from the University of Sheffield. In addition, some educational grants were given to the University, making it possible for high-calibre overseas science students from India to undertake Masters studies in Bio-medical Science, and several have gone on to complete a PhD. As time went on, grants were also awarded to university centres in other parts of the country.

Some BRET Fellows and other members of staff

Neena & Hannah

Raju

David

Kalyan

Basu

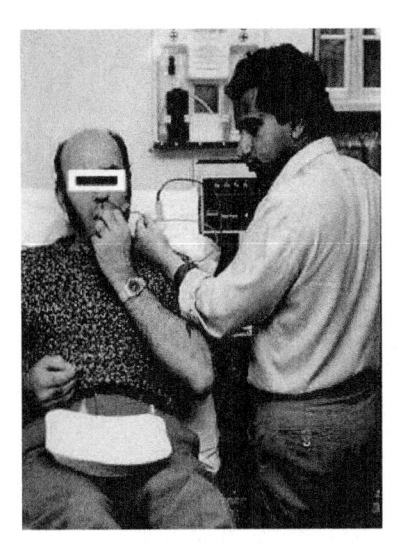

Pradip

I retired from clinical work on 30 March 2011 but continued almost full-time until 2014 with ongoing research and the teaching of University of Sheffield medical students posted to Rotherham. The changes in the research and the NHS environment required direction from younger and stronger hands, so the BRET Trustees invited Dr David Sanders to take on this role. David, now a Professor of Gastroenterology at Sheffield, is one of my former trainees who has gone on to establish a national and international reputation, assisted in part by grants from BRET. Under his direction, the charity has expanded greatly and now supports an increasing number of Research Fellows.

I was very fortunate to have worked in Rotherham before the new management system was introduced, and the achievement of targets, many of them futile, became the aim of the NHS. Today, individually-driven research would be virtually impossible to carry out in a district general hospital.

I guess I was the *right maverick* in the *right place* at the *right time*!

Projects Supported by BRET

(* KDB co-supervisor ± co-investigator **KDB co-investigator)

The list below gives you a flavour of the projects supported by BRET

PhD *(Three fund-holders, not named below, did not complete their PhD for personal reasons)*

Medicine-Physics

*Development of 24-hour ambulatory measurement of gastric acid

*Measurement of gastro-oesophageal reflux by non-invasive pH-metry

*Detection of pre-malignant changes in epithelium using impedance spectroscopy

*Systemic characterisation of gut blood flow

*Identification of abdominal adhesions by dynamic image registration

*Towards the non-invasive recognition of intra-abdominal adhesions

Symptom palliation of patients with oesophageal cancer

Medicine-Physiology

*Measurement of acid secretion by isolated gastric parietal cells

*Molecular mechanisms governing hematopoietic stem cell recruitment to injured murine intestinal micro-vessels in vivo / Do platelets recruit lymphocytes and stem cells following acute intestinal injury / Bile acid dysfunction in the intestine in irritable bowel syndrome

*Effects of *Helicobacter pylori* on endothelial cell proliferation and chemotaxis

Microbiology
Molecular analysis of the regulation of toxin production in the food poisoning bacterium *Staphylococcus aureus*

Analysis of the role of Sigma B in the control of toxin production, survival and pathogenicity of *Staphylococcus aureus*

*The role of ComH protein in *Helicobacter pylori* virulence

*Bacterial glycosylation: role in immune system modulation

History of Medicine
*The transformation of peptic ulcer disease into an epidemic: A study of underlying socio-economic factors

**The role of prostaglandin E2 in peptic ulcer disease CLEVER-1 and Mannose receptors mediate lymphocyte and dendritic cell recruitment to the liver [*Joint funding with CORE*]

University of Warwick – Engineering
*Non-invasive detection of bowel cancer from urine volatiles

MD
*Fibrinolysis in peptic ulcer disease

**Exploring new mechanisms responsible for idiopathic bile acid malabsorption and diarrhoea

The clinical influence of gluten exposure in Type-1 diabetes mellitus

Does the insertion of a percutaneous endoscopic gastrostomy (PEG) confer any quality of life benefit to either patients or their carers?

The role of FGF19 in the diagnosis and pathophysiology of primary bile acid diarrhoea

Taste studies in patients undergoing ENT treatment

Post-doctoral

*Investigations into regulation of small intestinal blood flow

*Phage treatment of bacterial infections

Characterisation of *Helicobacter pylori* TatD protein

Azathioprine pharmacogenetics in autoimmune hepatitis: Relationship to toxicity and to therapeutic efficacy

Role of osteopontin in lymphocyte recruitment in progressive alcoholic liver disease

Other grants but not specifically for higher degrees

Investigations into the regulation of small intestine blood flow

An investigation into the pathogenesis of gluten ataxia. The neurology of gluten sensitivity: Is the development of a B-cell response to TG6 the prelude to neuropathology, and can this constitute the primary autoimmune response in some patients?

The nature of a dietary factor that gives protection against duodenal ulceration and drug-induced ulceration

The effect of n-3 PUFA supplementation in nondiabetic patients with steatosis due to non-alcoholic fatty liver disease

Counselling Diploma

Endoscopic ablation of Barrett's oesophagus (equipment grant)

Five full bursary studentships for students from India to study a one-year MSc in Molecular Medicine

Contribution to new medical equipment

Confocal laser scanning for the detection and invasive depth estimation in early colorectal cancer (equipment grant)

Rotherham schools: After-school science clubs

Towards understanding the physical nature of extra-oesophageal refluxate: Laboratory-based studies on aerosol formation

The performance of faecal tumour M2-Pyruvate Kinas in the identification of oesophago-gastric cancer: Is a randomised controlled trial of screening in the normal population justified?

Aberrant expression of homing molecules on dendritic cells drives inflammation in Crohn's disease

Silent gastro-oesophageal reflux

Appendix

Some personal achievements

Rhodes Scholarship (1964-1967)

Rotherham Citizen of the Year Award (2000)

Hetenyi Gea Memorial Medal – Awarded by Hungarian Gastroenterology Society (2001)

Officer of the Most Excellent Order of the British Empire (OBE) (2002)

Honorary MD – University of Sheffield (2003)

Janssen Award for Outstanding Achievement in Clinical Gastroenterology (2003)

Freeman of the Borough of Rotherham (2004)

British Society of Gastroenterology (BSG) - Lifetime Achievement Award (2016)

OBE

Freeman

BSG

Printed in Great Britain
by Amazon